Jesus spells Freedom

Michael Green
Principal, St John's College, Nottingham

INTER-VARSITY PRESS

INTER-VARSITY PRESS

Inter-Varsity Fellowship
39 Bedford Square, London WC1B 3EY

© MICHAEL GREEN

First Edition August 1972
Reprinted October 1972

ISBN 0 85110 364 2

Printed in Great Britain
by Hunt Barnard Printing Ltd.,
Aylesbury, Bucks.

Contents

For Timothy, Sarah, Jennifer, Jonathan
and their generation.
Upon the responsible use we make of
our freedom
hangs the destiny of their world
in 2000 AD.

Preface

THERE IS no question facing contemporary man which is more relevant and more clamant than this: *how are we to use our freedom?*

We have, as a world, greater freedom than ever before. Politically, economically, socially, I suppose there has never been a time when most of the peoples of this planet enjoyed greater freedom. But never has there been a time when this freedom – indeed, the continued existence of the human race – was more at risk.

The next quarter of a century will be one of the most significant in the history of the world. We have the capacity, as a global society, to deal with the hunger problem that keeps over half the world in bondage; to survive the threat of nuclear destruction; to stay, before it is too late, the rash and selfish use of irreplaceable natural resources. Within this next quarter of a century either a peaceful mode of co-existence will be achieved between East and West or the world runs the gravest risk of an utter holocaust. Within this same period, the explosive demand for equality fomenting among subject nations in the world will burst, and the present revolutionary temper to be seen among young people everywhere will have had some decisive result. The outcome, who can tell? It all depends on how we use our freedom.

I have written this book out of the conviction that Jesus Christ holds the key to this intractable problem of the proper and responsible use of freedom. He was the most free man who ever lived. His life is the free man's model; his death the ultimate demonstration of what free love means. His risen power is the dynamic for changing men and societies. That is why I unashamedly call this book *Jesus Spells Freedom*. He does just that.

The church, however, scarcely exhibits freedom as its leading characteristic. It did in New Testament days. The apostle Paul could use successive chapters (5–8) of his 'Letter to the Romans' to show the way in which Christians are freed from guilt, evil habit, tradition, and the fear of death. Pretty comprehensive freedom, that; and all 'through Jesus Christ our Lord', as the final words of each of those chapters stress.

But does today's church show the unspeakable joy of an uncondemning conscience, secure in the knowledge that Christ has dealt with the accusing past?

Do Christians show by their actions and attitudes that the power of evil has been cracked in their lives, and that the risen life of Christ is at work in them, making them more like Jesus? All too rarely.

As for freedom from tradition, why, God forgive us, we Christians are in appalling bondage to what has been done in the past. 'As it was in the beginning, is now, and ever shall be, world without end, Amen' seems to be the motto of the church. When it comes to ecclesiastical conservatism we make the Pharisees look like radical reformers.

The fear of death still holds man in bondage, just as it has always done. But modern Christians show all too little of that exultant confidence in the face of death which marked the early church. How often is the note of triumph and joy struck at a Christian's funeral these days? Not often enough. In the early days of Christianity, men died joyfully, as those who were going to meet their dear Lord. Their friends escorted them to their burial as to a wedding. For they knew that death, that final curb on freedom, had itself suffered a death-blow through the resurrection of Jesus.

Certainly, then, the church has much to account for in its

fear of freedom, and its terrible failure – with shining exceptions – to exhibit that freedom in its life style. This failure may be partly due, at least, to the widespread ignorance of the New Testament among church people. They simply do not know what the Lord has to offer them, and accordingly remain beggars although they are inheritors of the deepest, most far-reaching liberty to be found anywhere. The remedy lies in looking afresh at the emancipation Jesus came to bring. That is what this small book tries to do. In writing it, I owe a lot to the privilege of taking part in a Mission to Cambridge University in 1971, to the help on the *Lolita* material in chapter three which has been given me by Tony Bridge, the Dean of Guildford, and to Rosemary, my wife, for all her advice on structure and detail, together with the ever helpful, ever courteous suggestions of Ronald Inchley of the IVP, without whose wisdom this book would have been a lot worse than it is. Dr David James has given generous help with proof-reading, that tedious task. Acknowledgment is also made for permission to quote from various letters and testimonies which have been included in this book.

The biblical quotations have been drawn sometimes from *The New English Bible*, sometimes from the *Revised Standard Version*, sometimes from *The Living Bible* and sometimes from my own translation.

Michael Green

1 Freedom for all?

'WHAT, NOT FREEDOM AGAIN? Surely that one's played out!'
But it isn't. You can't get away from it. Whether it's a case
of the housewife chained to the sink, dreaming of Women's
Lib., or the United Nations solemnly considering whether
the sovereignty of a member State has been infringed, the
importance of freedom can scarcely be exaggerated. The
politicians, hungry for votes, promise freedom. The makers
of deodorants, hungry for sales, do the same. In fact, one
widely-advertised anti-perspirant has been given the trade
name 'Feel Free'. Freedom remains an enigmatic but infinitely desirable good in an age which gets excited about few
other values. Freedom for all is undoubtedly the requirement.

We want the freedom to live: hence the persistent anti-
war pressure in the USA. We must have academic freedom,
so that knowledge can be pursued without Big Brother
surveillance by the government. We want freedom in
morals. Freedom in speech and expression goes without
saying, and accordingly any attempt at censorship is out.
Freedom for minorities is another cherished ideal; that is
why passionate feelings have been aroused throughout the
world by the plight of Jews in Russia. Perhaps most of all
we want the freedom from interference, from being strait-
jacketed by the bureaucracy; hence the uproar in Britain
when the military pundits in Whitehall tried to rub out an
ancient regiment such as the Argyll and Sutherland High-
landers in an army reshuffle, or when the politicians pro-

posed to eliminate a little village called Cublington and replace it with a third giant airport for London.

It would be easy and unnecessary to prolong examples of this sort of thing. The point is plain. We must be free of domination by others, be it political, economic or cultural: and that is why the world remains sickened by the rape of Czechoslovakia, the discrimination against men on the grounds of race and colour in South Africa, or any hint of neo-colonialism in the Third World.

When you stop to analyse it, does it not come to something like this? We want freedom in three main areas: in the intellectual area of our thought-life, so that we are free to seek truth wherever it may lead; in the practical area of our actions, so that we can live a fully satisfying life; and perhaps most of all in the central area of our inner being. Where is the clue to freedom so comprehensive as this? Let us examine these three areas of thought, action and being a little more closely.

Freedom in the realm of thought

We all want to be free to pursue truth, to believe it, and to express it. We are in favour, therefore, of a free Press and unbiased history books. But it is not so simple as that, is it?

Take the free Press for instance. In many countries the Press is an organ of government, and not free at all. In the West it is dominated by a handful of rich men who own the papers and wield tremendous power as they mould the opinions of their readers. How do we know what the truth is? Quite apart from the limitations of our own understanding, we are strongly influenced by our national, class and personal preconceptions and – let's admit it – prejudices. We are conned by propaganda: in most instances we have no means of verifying what we read or hear.

Where then is truth to be found? 'Ah,' you say, 'in objective reporting, in scientific, historical writing.' I'm sorry, but there is no such thing. When I report a happening, striving my best to be impartial, I am nevertheless recording my own impressions of what is significant in that event. I am making a selection: so is the historian and the reporter. And that selection is largely determined by our own pre-suppositions, education, character and so on. We must not look for objectivity in these areas. We will try to aim off to allow for our own and other people's special slant on things, but it is precarious to suppose that we have therefore arrived at the truth. What is the truth about freedom, for instance? You don't have to read philosophy for long to discover what a slippery concept 'truth' is – as elusive as soap in the bath. Two great words are in constant use among philosophers in connection with it: correspondence and coherence. A statement must *correspond* with reality if it is to be called true. But this is only a rough and ready guide; it is not a definition of truth. If a statement is really to qualify as being true, then it must *cohere* with all the rest of knowledge to make a sensible picture of the world.

Let's apply this to our quest for the truth about freedom. What world-picture makes sense of freedom? Well, there are basically only two to choose from, atheist and Christian.

The atheist account of truth and freedom

Most people these days have left God out of consideration. The picture of the world which had him in it seems curiously old-fashioned to us. Let's scrap the God hypothesis, then. What have we got left? An atheist world-view, which offers us two possible sets of impersonal factors to account for our world and our human nature.

Determinism

One possibility, I suppose, is some form of determinism. The world and man may simply be determined by fate or by the stars. Many people seem to be coming to believe this, if we may judge by the growth of horoscopes in all the papers and magazines. It's an interesting fact, actually, that when men push God out of the front door, fatalism or astrology slips in by the back. It has happened all through history. And the opposite holds good, too. When belief in a personal God comes in, the grip of astrology is broken. One of the great attractions of Christianity in the early days, when contemporary culture was even more determinist than it is now, was the freedom it brought from blind Destiny, *Atē* as the Greeks called her. Tatian, an able philosopher who became a Christian in the second century, expressed his liberation thus: 'We are above Fate, and instead of the demons which deceive, we have come to know one Master who does not deceive.'

A popular form of determinism these days is the chemical variety. Everything we do, on this view, is the result of previously-determined chemical changes in the brain. That chemical changes constitute the medium for our thinking processes is doubtless true, but no more satisfactory as a complete explanation than to imagine we have said all that is important about a man when we have analysed him into the chemical constituents of his body!

Anyway, if we were entirely determined by our internal chemistry, that would be the end of freedom and truth. For even if we were free (which we wouldn't be) to find truth (whatever that might be), we could not possibly *know* it was truth. Our minds would be chemically determined to operate in that way, and there would be, by definition, no possibility of altering their working. This is the decisive argument against all varieties of the determinist account of the world. If the determinist story were true, we could have no way of knowing it to be true. 'Truth' would simply mean the way we were predetermined to look at things.

Chance
The other possibility, on atheistical premises, would seem to be that the world and all that is in it, including human life and rationality, is due to chance. This view has received support in recent years from some geneticists who point out

the element of randomness in the fertilization of an ovum by one of thousands of spermatozoa. On this apparently random fusion the embryo depends for all its significant characteristics. There also seems to be randomness in the behaviour-patterns of protons and neutrons in an atom. But to move from these observations to the assertion that the whole of our lives is governed by chance is neither new nor true. Curiously enough, the ancient world, which was so ready to worship Fate, also had its worship of Chance. For all their fear that when your number came up you'd had it, which is determinism, they also sacrificed to the Goddess of Luck with the hope that 'it won't happen to me'. Of course, these are mutually contradictory ways of looking at the world, and you couldn't logically hold them both together: yet, paradoxically, people did, just as they do today. There is no reason to believe that either account is true. We have seen this in the case of Fate, but the same holds good for Chance. If Chance really is king, then there certainly is no truth to be discovered and no freedom to be enjoyed. For how could you arrive at truth when your mental processes in getting there were merely random? And if, by some fluke, you were to arrive, the truth itself would be merely the result of chance. And how could you be free in an entirely unstructured situation? Freedom wouldn't mean anything then. No, if the devotees of luck are right, then truth and freedom go out of the window.

But most people instinctively dismiss the advocates of chance and of determinism. We *know* that we have an element of choice and freedom in at least some aspects of our lives. We know, or if that is too strong a word, we have a strong hunch, that 'truth' is not just a meaningless noise. That is why we do not go along with these extreme attempts to get rid of values which we are convinced are real. And surely we are right.

Incoherence
Actually, however you present the atheist case, it leads to

incoherence. It has no adequate way of explaining how you get personal being in an impersonal world. Man comes from the impersonal, does he? He is the end-product (so far) of a development over millennia from amoebae floating helplessly in the sea of primeval chaos? Yet the fact remains that he can't treat others, let alone himself, as a mere collection of atoms. Man has immortal longings in his heart, and has had since time began, if we may judge from the burial customs of the earliest peoples. But, on the atheist's showing, immortality (unlike any other universal instinct) is an illusion. Man can pray; but there is no God to listen. He can talk of values; yet in the last analysis they are valueless, for from matter we come and to matter we go. There was no Creator in the beginning, and there is no destiny at the end. As for freedom, why, it is just a sick joke. For personal being is merely an irrelevant piece of flotsam on the vastness of space, time and the impersonal.

The Christian account of truth and freedom

The background

No, you don't get a coherent picture of truth or freedom by the atheist's path. But does the Christian explanation of them make any better sense? I believe it does. I think it is very significant that in the days when Christianity burst on the world an atomic theory was abroad which was based on atheistic presuppositions. Then, as today, there was growing despair, growing feelings that they were being dominated by dark, titanic forces over which men and their rulers had no control. There was an overpowering longing for freedom in men's hearts – freedom from war, hunger, domination, propaganda and so forth. As we have seen, *Atē*, Fate, and *Tuchē*, Chance, were held to control human affairs, and the results were obvious. Duty, failure and despair is the syndrome of fatalism. And many of the best fatalists of that day, the Stoics, ended it all in suicide. Living it up while you can is the creed of the believer in luck. And that didn't bring much satisfaction, either. Men cut loose in the thirties (under Caligula), in the sixties (under Nero), and in the nineties of the first century (under Domitian) in licence and a mad pursuit of pleasure which makes today's permissive society look positively staid. Yet they found themselves enslaved by their free pleasures, as a drunkard is by his bottle. No exit to freedom that way. But once men and women came face to face with Jesus, who once described himself to his disciples as 'the truth', then they found a liberation they had not dreamed of. It had many sides, this liberation, but it certainly included freedom in the realm of thought. And it still does.

Human reason

Christianity says something like this. 'Of course your understanding is limited. Not only by the prejudice and ignorance which you are happy to confess, but by the sheer fact of your creatureliness, which you are so anxious to repudiate. The fact is, you are finite. You are the creation of an infinite and personal God. God! Let that thought sink into your mind. Then you won't be surprised if the finite can't take in the infinite. You won't fondly imagine that your unaided human reason will take you all the way. You won't be so arrogant as to suppose that the truth is no bigger than your understanding of it. You will cease to measure everything by the hopelessly inadequate scales of your reason.'

Not, of course, that you will be irrational. Reason is a God-given faculty, and is to be valued enormously. But you must put it in its right place. And the right place is certainly not when it says, like a blind man in a sunlit garden, 'Anything I can't see doesn't exist.' Paul wrote a letter about 55 AD to some Christians at Corinth who remained, after their conversion, unduly opinionated about the importance of the human reason. 'Who knows', he asks, 'what a man is but the man's own spirit within him? In the same way, only the Spirit of God knows what God is. This is the Spirit that we have received from God. . . . '[1] That makes sense, doesn't it? It is only my humanity which enables me to understand what it is to be a man. My tame black rabbit couldn't get there in a month of Sundays, however hard it tried. But if, for the sake of argument, I could put a human spirit in the mind of that rabbit, it would begin to understand something of my mind. Now what is impossible for us to do to rabbits, is not impossible for God to do to us. He made us. He can reveal himself to us, and the Christian claim is that he has done so. The job of our human intellect is not to try to pierce the incognito of the Infinite: we shall fail as miserably as the rabbit. But rather to respond gladly to the person of the Creator, and use our God-given powers of reason to get to grips with the revelation of himself that he has generously given us.

God's intervention

And what is that? It is a long story. It goes back to the very beginning. Back to the time when God made man in his own image of freedom with the ability to know and love him – an ability that inevitably carried with it a dangerous corollary: man could choose to hate and reject him. And that, by and large, is how man has acted down the centuries. Is it not like that today? Indeed, is it not like that with you, unless you are one of those who has already come to terms with your gracious and loving Maker by putting your life unreservedly in his hands?

Yes, back at the beginning, man began to go his own way, and that way spelt ruin. Not freedom, as men thought, but bondage to self-will.

How was God to break into a situation like that, when the very people he had made didn't want to know about him, and preferred the illusory freedom of independence to the reality of relationship with him? Well, what would you do if you were in God's shoes? I suppose you might teach them by circumstances: the harsh facts of life might help to bring

[1] 1 Corinthians 2 : 11, 12.

home to them the realities of the situation. God tried that. And the harsh realities of life included a flood, a captivity in Egypt and another in Babylon. They certainly learnt the hard way.

Another thing you might do is to try direct instruction. God did just that. He did it through men who lived close to him, prophets as we call them. Their teaching was hard hitting and practical, and the whole purpose of it was to bring people back to putting God in the centre of their lives. Read J. B. Phillips' translation of Isaiah, Amos, Hosea and Micah, entitled *Four Prophets*, if you want to see in contemporary, stirring English what it was about these men in the eighth century BC that made them some of the greatest moral and religious teachers the world has ever seen.

Truth incarnate

But I suppose there is one other thing you might do if you really cared passionately enough that these men you had made should gain the freedom of knowing and obeying the truth. You *might* do it, if you were prepared to pay the price. You might come yourself, and show them, mightn't you? God tried that, too. In what happened in Bethlehem's cradle, on the Mount of the Sermon, on the cross of Calvary, I see to the heart of reality: I see the truth. 'In him', said the apostle Paul, writing about Jesus, 'dwells all the fulness of the Godhead in bodily form.'[2] We shall pause on the breathless audacity of a claim like that in the next chapter: let it go for the moment. But think of what it means. It is saying that all we can know of the truth, of final explanations, of ultimate reality, confronts us in Jesus of Nazareth.

I used to puzzle about Jesus' trial before Pilate. You remember the point when Pilate asked, quizzically, 'What is truth?'[3] and got no answer. 'Why didn't Jesus tell him?' I

[2] Colossians 2 : 9.
[3] John 18 : 38.

wondered. And now I think I see. There wasn't anything Jesus could say about the truth that would help. The truth was present with Pilate that day, standing right in front of him. The truth was Jesus – *is Jesus*. Had he not once said to his followers: 'I am the Truth'?[4]

That is not to denigrate other aspects of truth, such as the importance of what the scientist is doing when he seeks to uncover more of the mysteries of our world; nor to despise the value of the psychologist who seeks to understand the depths of human nature. No. It is simply to say that in Jesus of Nazareth final truth has taken personal form. The truth about what God is like is to be found here. The truth about what human nature should be like is to be found here. The truth about freedom and love and uprightness of character are all to be found here, in this personal embodiment of ultimate reality, Jesus Christ.

The implications

I am not asking you to *believe* that just at the moment. It would be wrong to believe it without overwhelming evidence. I shall say something about that evidence later. It is certainly the most fantastic claim that could possibly be made about anyone. But Christians are committed to it. Let us have a look and see what it would mean. Just supposing it were true, would it offer us freedom in the realm of thought?

For one thing, it would make sense of values. Beauty and love and goodness would, on this showing, find their natural point of integration in him, the truth. They would not appear, as on the atheist view they must, as surds for which one has to find some explanation in a world that had no origin, no meaning, no goal. They would represent aspects of the self-disclosure of God, the personal Creator God, who showed himself decisively in Jesus Christ. There and nowhere else, unutterable beauty, unspeakable goodness, undying love unite. In the same way, we should not

[4] John 14 : 6.

have to find tortuous arguments to explain how our reason evolved from inorganic origins which had no reason directing them: reason would take its place as a gift of God, to be thankfully received and used – not to be erected as an idol and worshipped. Our vitality, our ability to communicate, would derive from a living Creator who has seen fit to communicate with his creatures, and wants them to get in touch with him. It certainly makes a coherent picture.

This leads into a second important result, if the Christian story is true. It will mean that you can enter into your work whole-heartedly, in the light of the creativity you derive from God. Work need not, then, be a bind, or a mere way of getting money, but a calling. Your very science will be imbued with the purpose of 'thinking God's thoughts after him'. Your social concern will be the deeper because you are trying to help one of God's creatures, whom he made, for whom he died, whom he loves just as much as he loves you.

What's more, if this Christian understanding of freedom and truth is accepted, it means you don't have to live, as it were, in a pair of trousers – torn between personal, meaningful, loving relationships on the one hand, and the recognition, on the other hand, that it is all pointless, for we come from plankton soup and have no future except dissolution. You inhabit a unified world, where nature and man both owe their origin to God.

It will mean, too, that you can face life without excessive anxiety. So often our freedom of thought is crippled by fear. For the Christian this need not be so. For he is in touch with the source of his very being, the God who made him, who came to this world for him, who told him not to be afraid, and who even goes to the lengths of coming to live in him so that 'the peace of God may set guard over your hearts and minds through Christ Jesus'.[5] That peace makes free men of us.

[5] Philippians 4 : 7.

Perhaps best of all, if the Christian story stands up to critical scrutiny, it means that I need never fear the truth. For the truth has invaded my world in search of me. The truth was crucified for me and rose for me. I need never be afraid of the truth from whatever source it comes. I need never resort to obscurantism and pretence, because every bit of truth I am shown gives me yet deeper insight into the wonder of reality whose personal face is Jesus Christ. No split personality, then; no suppressed war between my religious beliefs, kept locked up safely in one compartment, and the rest of my world view, which must not be allowed to infect them! No, the truth is one, for God is one. And the truth, which came to look for me in Jesus Christ, is never going to hurt me. I can and shall welcome it wherever I find it, giving thanks to the God and Father of my Lord Jesus Christ.

There it is then. Just two accounts of the world. The one based on the view that there is no personal, rational, loving source to the world: the other that there is. You must ask yourself which account corresponds better with the facts as you assess them. Which, in your view, gives the most coherent picture of the world? You are free to choose.

Freedom in the field of action

This is the cry alike of the student and of the toddler, the diplomat and the columnist in the *International Times*. We all want freedom of behaviour, freedom to do what we like with no Big Brother breathing down our necks. Freedom from constraint, from legalistic rules, from the traditional. . . .

Yet here again there are acknowledged difficulties, whatever our philosophy of life. You don't need to be a burned-out playboy to know that unbridled licence leads to uncontrolled anarchy. Prudential considerations drive each of us, atheist and Christian alike, to recognize that the exercise of my personal freedom must not inhibit the next man's, if freedom is really to be for all and not just for the few. Very well then: the conclusion is inescapable. Freedom must be partnered by responsibility. But responsibility to whom? To what? To 'them'? To the party bosses or the egg-heads? To my own idea of what is best for others? Or the ideas of the crowd I mix with?

The atheist account of responsible freedom

The atheist normally tries to handle this problem by means of calculating what course of action would bring the greatest happiness or good to the greatest number. At least that's what he says he does. But I wonder. I was discussing this once with a very vocal group of socialist students in London. They were passionately advocating the ending of the war in Vietnam, which was the current anti-establishment cause. I asked them why, on their declared atheist presuppositions, they should care about men dying in Vietnam. They replied, 'We get a kick out of it.' I said to them, 'I submit to you that you don't protest about this cause just because you get a kick out of it.' They said, 'Well, perhaps not. We are concerned for the greatest happiness of the greatest number, and that's why we are against the war.' I said to them, 'Did you really sit down and consider the greatest happiness of the greatest number when you were deciding to stage your protest?' They had the honesty to admit that they did not. 'Why, then, do you care about Vietnam?' I asked. 'After all, the Vietnamese are only purposeless bundles of atoms, bound for extinction sooner or later. Why not sooner? Why get so worked up about them?' They had no answer. I went on something like this: 'I'll tell you why you care. You care because you are human, because you know what it is to be loving and compassionate and concerned about justice. You care because, although you have written off God with the top of your head, he exists, and he is so concerned to know you and to share your life that he has left his imprint of love and compassion on your heart. You care because behind the brotherhood of

25

man which you enthuse over, there lies not an unseeing void, as you maintain, but the fatherhood of God.'

The Christian account of responsible freedom

How does a Christian handle the problem of responsible use of freedom? He seeks to act in a truly human way. 'Oh,' you say, 'then he is just the same as the humanist?' Not quite. His actions may, and often will, be identical with the humanist's; and it is important that Christians and humanists should take joint action for righting the variety of social, political and economic injustices to be found in every nation. But they will have quite different springs of action. The atheist will love because he happens to be a kind fellow, or because he has an irrational but deep conviction that love is better than hate. The Christian will welcome his concern, but will point out that on his views it would be just as logical to hate as to love, to destroy as to build up, provided one could get away with it. Why not, if there is no God, no absolute standards, no future life? Why not? But if the Christian story is true, there is every reason for what I have called 'acting in a truly human way'. And the strongest of those reasons is Jesus Christ.

There has been only one fully human being. All others are sub-human. The Ideal is not beyond us: he has lived. And he continues to influence and guide the actions of his followers. Just think of him for a moment. Was there ever a man so free?

He came from a working-class family, yet was entirely free of inverted snobbery. He was brought up in a strict Jewish home, yet was entirely free from prejudice. He belonged to a subject race, yet he remained in complete control of his circumstances. Strong believer though he was in the Old Testament, he nevertheless felt free to reinterpret its general precepts in certain individual cases.[6] Here was

---

[6] See, for instance, his attitude to the woman taken in adultery (John 8: 1–11), when the Old Testament penalty was death (Deuteronomy 22: 22ff.).

no slave to the system. He could say, 'Think not that I have come to abolish the law and the prophets; I have come not to abolish them but to fulfil them.'[7]

Free from fear, he was also free from arrogance. He had no taboos, no chips on the shoulder, no pride, and no mealy-mouthed humility either. What a free man! He never drew a sword or cast a vote, yet his teaching has been one of the most potent weapons for reform of community life all over the world ever since. He never freed a slave or enfranchised a woman, yet his attitudes and teaching were the inspiration of the great social reforms in the West which righted both these injustices. He never functioned outside Palestine, yet his precepts and his attitudes to men and women of other races have led to the world-wide missionary movement and the breakdown of class and colour prejudice. He was free to hold on to his life and feather his nest, had he chosen to do so.

Instead he died at the age of 33. Why? Not because the big batallions caught up with him at last, nor because he was enmeshed in a net from which he could not escape. But because he was carrying out his own paradoxical teaching, 'The man who holds on to his life will lose it. The man who is prepared to lose his life for my sake and the sake of the Good News, will find it.'[8]

Think of Jesus at his trial, bound and blindfolded in the courtroom. Was he the prisoner? Or were they? Prisoners all of jealousy, pride, envy, greed, selfrighteousness and hate: but he was free, utterly free. 'You would have no power over me unless it had been given you from above'[9] was his calm rejoinder to the threats of the man who was trying him on a capital charge. Jesus was free all right.

Or think of him at Calvary. The others, as they were executed, cursed and swore, and no doubt did their best to kick and bite. He said, 'Father, forgive them; for they do

[7] Matthew 5 : 17.
[8] Mark 8 : 34f.
[9] John 19 : 11.

not know what they are doing.'[1] Who was the free man in that situation?

Jesus is the goal and the measuring-stick of Christian freedom. In him we have, so to speak, a pencilled-in outline drawing of the responsible use of freedom, for us to ink in according to the circumstances in which we are placed. We know enough about Jesus to be able to extrapolate with some assurance from the way he behaved during his lifetime to the way he would want us to behave now. We shall try to examine some of the ways that would work out in the final chapter. For the moment, the broad principle is clear. Once I am bound by love and obedience to the supremely free man, Jesus of Nazareth, I am free from the rigid rules of law on the one hand, and from moral anarchy in the exercise of my freedom on the other. And that is responsible freedom indeed.

Freedom in the realm of being

It's difficult to put this into words. But is it not true that at times we are all disappointed with ourselves? Disenchanted? Nauseated? We long to be free to develop, to be what we euphemistically call 'our true selves', to escape from convention, to form valid and deep relationships, to get the very most out of life. And it doesn't quite work out.

Man in chains
Our personal freedom allows us to fall into bad habits but not into good ones. There's a curious lack of freedom in our inner being, which seems to fetter the good and encourage the bad. How often we have to admit, ruefully, after some lapse which we regret, 'I don't know what made me do it.' But we show our bondage by doing it over and over again. Of course, we very much resent any suggestion that we are

[1] Luke 23 : 34.

not free, or that we cannot liberate ourselves. But it is none the less true. Jimi Hendrix, the famous entertainer who committed suicide, once said, 'Do I seem free? If I'm free it's because I'm always running.' In the end he didn't run far enough to get away from himself.

It's been like that all down the years. Human nature has not been free to maximize its potential. Herodotus, the 'Father of History', spoke in the fifth century BC of a distressing feature in human affairs 'that we aim at so much but fail to achieve it'. Seneca, the Stoic philosopher who taught the Emperor Nero and wrote some of the most noble moral discourses, was nevertheless a slave to wealth. He confessed, 'I am in the grip of habits that fetter me. I cannot escape from the pits into which I have fallen unless an arm from above should rescue me.' Ovid, a contemporary of Jesus, was a charming, fluent poet, but a slave to the sensuality which in due course ruined his career. He wrote, wrily, 'I see the better course, and I approve it. I follow the worse!'

This is a theme which has fascinated writers of every sort. You find it in philosophers like Martin Buber, with his complaint, 'Who can change that intractable thing, human nature? There is a tragedy at the heart of things.' You find it among playwrights, like Albert Camus. His *Caligula* is an extended study in freedom. Caligula, the despotic ruler of the Roman Empire (at that time practically coextensive with the whole known world), wields absolute power. 'You see in me the one free man in the whole Roman Empire. You should be glad to have at last amongst you an emperor who points the way to freedom.' Absolute freedom. But it led to absolute selfishness, absolute folly and absolute ruin. The play ends with the crazed emperor, in a moment of sanity, saying, 'I have chosen a wrong path, a path that leads to nothing. My freedom isn't the right one. . . . ' He cannot stand the reflection of himself in the mirror, hurls a stool at it, shatters the glass, and with a wild laugh turns to face his murderers.

You find that modern music is much concerned with this same theme of the inability of man to control himself, the surd of wickedness which lies in every man's inner being and which cannot be eradicated by any amount of education, social conditioning, improved housing or psychiatry. Justin Haywood of the Moody Blues wrestled with this issue in 'Question', as recently as 1970.

'Why do we never get an answer when we're knocking on the door
With a thousand million questions about hate and death and war?
'cause when we stop and look around us there is nothing that we need
In a world of persecution that is whirling in its greed.
Why do we never get an answer when we're knocking on the door?'

The answer is not just a changed society, and Haywood realizes this. A changed society needs changed people. Perhaps that is why he brings in this haunting chorus,

'I'm looking for someone to change my life. I'm looking for a miracle in my life.'

Unless there is that miracle, the outlook is depressing. Only the previous year the group King Crimson had produced two terrifying records, 'Twenty-first century schizoid man' and 'Epitaph'. The first sets the scene:

'Cat's foot, iron claw, neuro-surgeons scream for more at paranoia's poison door; twenty-first century schizoid man.

Blood rack, barbed wire, politicians' funeral pyre, innocents raped with napalm fire; twenty-first century schizoid man.

Death seed, blind man's greed, poet's starving children bleed, nothing he's got he really needs; twenty-first century schizoid man.'

The second draws the conclusion:

'The wall on which the prophets wrote is cracking at the seams.
Upon the instruments of death the sunlight brightly gleams.
When every man is torn apart with nightmares and with dreams –
Will no-one lay the laurel wreath as silence drowns the screams?

Between the iron gates of fate the seeds of time are sown,
And watered by the deeds of those who know and who are known;
Knowledge is a deadly friend when no-one sets the rules.
The fate of all mankind, I see, is in the hands of fools.

Confusion will be my epitaph
As I crawl a cracked and broken path
If we make it, we can all sit back and laugh –
But I fear tomorrow I'll be crying,
Yes, I fear tomorrow I'll be crying.'

If King Crimson are too depressing for our liking, the same theme comes at us from other quarters in the pop world. Leonard Cohen's 'Bird on a Wire' is a case in point:

'Like a bird on a wire,
Like a drunk in some midnight choir,
I have tried, in my way, to be free.'

And Joni Mitchell gets the flavour of the emptiness of it all:

'And the seasons, they go round and round
And the painted ponies go up and down,
We're captives on a carousal of time.'

The theologians also stress this same uncomfortable

truth, that we cannot live up to our lights, try as we may. 'The congenital weakness of human nature', wrote J. S. Whale, 'is the submerged rock on which the complacent claims of our optimistic humanism are shattered.' The apostle Paul had put it a lot more crisply 2000 years ago with this piece of autobiography: 'Though the will to do good is there, the deed is not. The good which I want to do, I fail to do; but what I do is the wrong which is against my will. . . .'[2]

That is your experience and mine. It is true of everyone. So proud of our freedom, we are defeated day after day. One man is in bondage to snobbery. Another to lust. One has awful home relationships. Another is so self-satisfied that he is blind to the faults which other people see writ large in his character. We are not free after all. The tragedy of the human situation is that we are enslaved to the very forces which we detest in others and repudiate for ourselves, but from which we cannot escape. Evil deeds, evil words, evil thoughts, and a wrong attitude to the God who gave us life. He is excluded by deliberate choice or plain neglect. I am forced to conclude that it is not the next person, but *I* who am the man in chains. I am not, after all, free in my inner being.

What is worse, I am responsible for this state of affairs. I am responsible for the bitter words that I say, the spiteful thoughts I cherish and the greedy, selfish things I do. I am responsible for the attitude of defiance I have taken up towards God. 'This is the judgment, that the light has come into the world, and men loved darkness rather than light, because their deeds were evil.'[3] That describes me well enough. I am guilty.

It would be pleasant to wash my hands of the whole affair, to get it behind me. Pontius Pilate tried to do this when he ostentatiously ordered a basin and towel and washed his hands to signify that he was innocent of Jesus'

[2] Romans 7 : 19.
[3] John 3 : 19.

death. But the responsibility was not so easily shelved, and 'crucified under Pontius Pilate' remains in the Creed as his epitaph.

There is a moving variant on this theme in Shakespeare's *Macbeth*. Lady Macbeth, after the murder, cannot quieten her guilty conscience. As she sleep-walks, rubbing her hands together in an imaginary washing, an attendant observes, 'It is an accustomed action with her, to seem thus washing her hands: I have known her continue in this a quarter of an hour.'

In her sleep Lady Macbeth cries, 'Out, damned spot! out, I say! . . . Here's the smell of the blood still: all the perfumes of Arabia will not sweeten this little hand. Oh, oh, oh!'

The doctor observes, 'What a sigh is there! The heart is sorely charged. . . . This disease is beyond my practice.'

Man set free

It is at this point that the Christian gospel is supremely relevant. There is no other message in the world that can finally give rest to a guilty conscience. If it be true that God Almighty has made himself responsible for my wrongdoing, then I need not bear it on my conscience a moment longer. If he says 'your sins and your iniquities I will remember no more',[4] then I can indeed forget them. To return to the 'blood' imagery of Lady Macbeth and Pilate, although my sins may be like scarlet and crimson, as Isaiah put it,[5] they can be as white as snow. What Pilate could not do, what Lady Macbeth could not do, in evading guilt, has been done by Christ on the cross, absorbing guilt. As man, he stood in for men there at the place of our greatest need. As God, what he did there has lasting effects. Thus the apostle John can say: 'If we say we have no sin, we deceive ourselves, and the truth is not in us. If we confess our sins, God is faithful and just, and will forgive our sins and cleanse us from all unrighteousness.' And how does this

[4] Hebrews 8 : 12; 10 : 17; *cf.* Jeremiah 31 : 34.
[5] Isaiah 1 : 18.

come about? 'The blood of Jesus Christ, his Son, goes on cleansing us from all sin.'[6] His 'blood', that is to say his life laid down in death for us on the cross, can and does cleanse the conscience from guilt, from the objective state of being in the wrong with God, which is where each one of us is situated.

The imagery of rescue through the 'blood' of another is foreign to us these days, except in war, but it is not difficult to see what it meant to a people who were used to the practice of animal sacrifice. For two thousand years the Jews had been offering animals in sacrifice to the Lord, but still they could not get rid of that guilty conscience. As a New Testament writer steeped in the sacrificial system put it, 'In these sacrifices year after year sins are brought to mind, because sins can never be removed by the blood of bulls and goats.'[7] Of course not. Personal wrongdoing can be put right only by a person. And those old sacrifices pointed to the way in which God himself would intervene in the person of Jesus Christ and in a human body bear responsibility for human sin, at the cost of his own life, no less. In contrast, then, to the Old Testament priest who 'stands performing his service daily and offering time after time the same sacrifices, which can never remove sins . . . Christ offered for all time one sacrifice for sins, . . . and where these have been forgiven, there is no longer any offering for sin.'[8] The task is done, and does not need repeating.

Let me close this chapter by a letter which I have just received. It was written by a tough lumberjack, a man who had had a good education and background and had gone to pieces through alcohol. Christian people had kept in touch with him and succeeded in bringing him, much against his will, to a conference at which I was present. He had a most uncomfortable time there, as he kicked violently

[6] 1 John 1 : 7-9.
[7] Hebrews 10 : 3, 4.
[8] Hebrews 10 : 11-13, 18.

against everything that was said. By the conclusion of that weekend he had come to the end of himself, and he poured out his heart to God in honest repentance, doubts and all. His letter ran as follows:

'I purposely have not written to you until now because I wanted to see if what happened to me would last. It has lasted!

'I left you that night and went downstairs to join some of the congregation . . . and a couple of alcoholic friends. There was a deep calm in my guts. I immediately told my friends that I had given my heart, my soul, my body and my "gizzard" to Jesus Christ. What really got through to me was the love of God through you, Michael. I know now that even if I'd been the only one in the world that needed help, Christ would have died for me. I have been thanking him every day since.

'My craving for alcohol and cigarettes instantly left me that night and I have had no desire for either of them since. My resentments are gone, and my fears, but I find that when I'm not watching they can sometimes creep up on me again when I get to "stinkin-thinkin" as we call it in A.A. So I have to keep on coming back to him. But the big difference is now I have him to come back to . . . My wife, from whom I have been separated, does not want to have anything to do with me. But a whole new relationship is opening up with my three kids.'

That man has found freedom in Christ, freedom in the depths of his being. The freedom available for him is available for all.

2 Free man's model

WE HAVE BEEN MAKING some enormous assumptions in the previous chapter. That Jesus Christ actually existed; that he was the Son of God; that he rose from the dead and is alive today. There are three for a start. It is high time to examine the evidence. For the one thing we cannot abide these days, and rightly, is unreality. Long-accepted answers cut no ice. People want reality and they want it now.

The quest for reality

This hunger for what is real is one of the causes behind the craze for experimenting with drugs. In an interesting article on 'LSD and the Search for God' Dr Allan Cohen, one of the originators of the psychedelic movement, wrote:

> 'Young people are free to conquer the world – and they don't want it. Material prosperity has not made life meaningful. The hunger for love and real meaning are the forces behind the psychedelic revolution.'

Cohen joins Meher Baba in concluding that the drug experience is as far removed from reality as a mirage from water. But the search is real enough.

We want the truth about life. Well, Christians claim that Jesus Christ is the truth about life, that this man who has straddled the world like a colossus during the nineteen hundred years since his birth is the clue to what ultimate reality is all about. Such, as we saw in the last chapter, is part of the Christian claim.

But the very magnitude of the claim raises a host of questions. Not least among them is this: where are we to find the Jesus who is supposed to have this liberating effect? Did he ever live? Is he for real?

Is Jesus real?

This question has recently been raised insistently in the pop world, through the rock opera 'Jesus Christ, Superstar'.

> 'Jesus Christ, Jesus Christ? Who are you? What have you sacrificed? Jesus Christ, Superstar, do you think you're what they say you are?'

That is what the crowd wonder in the opera. Judas Iscariot becomes disillusioned with Jesus and the central position he occupies in his own teaching. He complains perceptively,

> 'You've begun to matter more
> Than the things you say.'

What Tim Rice and Andrew Lloyd Webber raise in their work is an entirely honest enquiry: who is Jesus? They do not in the opera give more than a hint as to the answer, for the simple reason that they do not know it, and are too honest to write beyond their own experience. That is why they stop at the cross, and have nothing on the resurrection. They are not sure if it is true or not. Their aim is 'to strip away the myth from the man', and the authentic nature of their search has struck a responsive chord with a vast audience in America, Europe and the Far East. Not only the writers, but the listeners are interested in the real Jesus.

The Founder of Christianity

Recently Professor C. H. Dodd published a book called *The Founder of Christianity*. It is all about Jesus. The author is an outstanding British New Testament scholar, and was chairman of the team of experts who translated *The New English Bible*. His book represents the careful, reverent fruit of a life-time's work. In it he sets out, with the ordinary reader in mind, to 'strip away the myth from the man', and find the real Jesus. He finds him in the pages of the New Testament record.

But did you see the review of this book by Professor H. R. Trevor-Roper in the *Spectator*?[1] Splashed sensationally across the front page, along with a macabre cartoon of Jesus crucified, are quotations from the review. 'The plain fact is that we know nothing about the historical Jesus . . . The Gospels, after all, tell us a lot of palpable rubbish . . . The Church created Christ.' Now that, I submit, is the reaction of a man who wilfully evades the real Jesus.

Trevor-Roper tells us that Paul of Tarsus, the earliest of the New Testament writers, records no concrete historical facts about the life of Jesus: 'of the life of Christ on earth he says nothing.' In point of fact Paul records Jesus' Davidic descent;[2] he alludes to his birth from a virgin;[3] he tells us of his conformity to the law,[4] his teaching on marriage,[5] his institution of the Lord's Supper (including the very words he used).[6] He tells us a great deal about his death;[7] he insists again and again upon his resurrection,[8] and he sets Jesus forth as our example for humility, for self-sacrifice and for obedience.[9]

But Trevor-Roper is a Professor of *Modern* History. He can be forgiven for being imperfectly informed about the writings of Paul. After all, they are outside his period! However, when he affects doubt over even the historical existence of Jesus – thus neglecting at one fell swoop the

[1] *Spectator*, 23 January 1971.
[2] Romans 1 : 3.
[3] Galatians 4 : 4.
[4] *Ibid.*
[5] 1 Corinthians 7 : 10.
[6] 1 Corinthians 10 : 16f.; 11 : 23ff.
[7] *E.g.* 1 Corinthians 1 : 18; Galatians 3 : 1, *etc.*
[8] 1 Corinthians 15; Philippians 2 : 9; Colossians 3 : 1.
[9] Philippians 2 : 4–11.

evidence of the non-Christian sources, Josephus, Tacitus and Suetonius; when he claims that the Gospels, or rather something approaching them, were not written until the beginning of the second century in order to 'create a personality behind the myth'; when he maintains that 'no Gospel text can be traced, even indirectly, back beyond the fourth century AD', then Professor Trevor-Roper is displaying not merely culpable ignorance but rank prejudice. He clearly does not want to know about the real Jesus. He prefers to run away from the evidence.

It so happens that we have a fragment of John's Gospel, the latest of the four Gospels, which is confidently dated by the palaeographers before 125 AD. We have copies of all four Gospels from the third quarter of the second century. And we have manuscripts of practically all the New Testament by the year 200. The gap between the originals and the earliest copies we possess is not much more than a century, less by far than with any other ancient document. The gap in Tacitus' case (a Roman historian of the first century AD) amounts to some 800 years; in Thucydides' case (a Greek historian of the fifth century BC) it is as much as 1500 years between autograph and first extant copy. Yet nobody doubts the substantial accuracy of the text of these classical writings; nobody is foolish enough to suggest that the history they relate is entirely mythical. It is only in the case of the New Testament, where the issues are so crucial, that sceptics have recourse to this card. And a very bad card it is. For we have thousands of manuscripts of the New Testament, written in dozens of languages from all over the known world. Their combined testimony to the text of the documents is so overwhelming that New Testament scholars do not even waste their time in suggesting conjectural emendations to the text. It is too firmly assured for that. No, it is not the supposed unreliability of the New Testament text that has led Professor Trevor-Roper to make such bizarre and unguarded accusations: it is, I fancy, the picture of Jesus there disclosed in all his appeal but in all his challenge which has led him to decide that it must be attacked.

We cannot avoid the challenge of the real Jesus by damning the evidence of the Gospels: they have survived attack by edict, fire, calumny, proscription and ridicule for many centuries and their credit stands as high as ever. Back, then, to the documents themselves, if we are to discover some of his real characteristics. Here are three which run through every strand of the material about him which has come down to us.

The human attractiveness of Jesus

World-wide appeal

One of the truly astonishing things about Jesus is the way in which he has struck people of every age and class and colour and country as the ideal man. He has dominated art, literature and music for most of the time from his day to ours. Even those who have no time for the church cannot evade the spell of Jesus – witness Mahatma Gandhi, Lord Boothby and J. M. Allegro.

In this twentieth century people are flocking to Jesus Christ in countries as far apart and cultures as diverse as South America, Ethiopia, Russia, Korea and Indonesia. In Indonesia there is a massive move over from nominal Islam to Christ: ask any pastor what his problem is, and he will tell you, 'Too many converts.' In Tanzania the Anglicans alone are building two churches a week to accommodate the growth rate of the church which has for many years exceeded 14% annually. The growth of the Baptists in Russia has been widely recognized in recent years, and the revival of the Orthodox Church there is no less remarkable. All the young priests, of course, are men who have been indoctrinated in atheism, so their commitment to the Christian ministry is hardly thoughtless or traditional! Less well known is the situation in Ethiopia. A handful of Protestants left that country in 1936 as a result of the Abyssinian war. They left behind them some forty wavering converts. They were completely cut off during the ensuing years until after the Second World War. When the missionaries got back in 1946, wondering if they would have to begin again from scratch, they found a flourishing church of 40,000. Today there are over 300,000.

Ideal man

What accounts for the world-wide appeal of Jesus? Perhaps it is that he really is the ideal for human life. He was, of course, no Western man, but an inhabitant of the Middle East. No privileged person, he, but a manual worker, able to mix as easily and naturally with kings as with social outcasts. He came from a big family and lived in a simple home with no lavatory, no hot and cold. We read of his getting exhausted in the service of others, but never of his turning them away; we see him parched by the heat of the sun, but not too thirsty to converse with a needy woman and to help her. We find him weeping at the tomb of his friend Lazarus, in sympathy for the family and in affection for the dead man. We hear of the little children climbing on his knee. His great compassion for all and sundry shines out through the Gospel account, and it is very attractive. It makes no difference whether you are one of thousands in a vast, hungry crowd, or whether you are the sick child of a nobleman, or a frightened theologian creeping in by night – in each case Jesus cares, and shows his care by compassionate action. He could dine with a self-righteous Pharisee, and allow a woman of the streets to slip in and wash his feet with her tears of penitence and wipe them with her hair.

Non-aligned politically, he could attract and hold the loyalty of the conventional conservative like Nicodemus, the collaborator like Zacchaeus and the Leftist like Simon the Zealot. He was at home in any company. His joy, his vitality, his passionate uprightness, his constant outgoing care, and the power that marked both his teaching and his

41

actions – all this made virtue front-page news. He talked about the love of God that was like a woman searching for one lost coin, or a shepherd tracking down one lost sheep. That's how much every individual matters to God. And he didn't just talk like that. He lived like that.

The religious rabbi of those days tended to despise the common people. Needless to say, they returned the compliment with interest. Rabbi Akiba began as one of the common people, the Great Unwashed who, almost by definition, were incapable of keeping God's law. He used to say, 'I wish I had one of those scholars. I would bite him like an ass.' 'You mean, like a dog?' asked his disciples. 'Like an ass,' replied Akiba. 'An ass's bite breaks the bone. A dog's does not.' What was Jesus' attitude? He broke the class barrier. He would touch the untouchable – lepers. He would equally heal in the royal family. His teaching was directed both towards the teachers of the law and the outcasts from the law. The pious Jew would thank the Almighty daily that he was not born a woman: Jesus both cared for women and appealed to them. In the long run, their loyalty held when the men ran away.

Unique teacher
The human attractiveness of Jesus was and remains worldwide. His influence was, and remains, unparalleled. His teaching was and still is unequalled, and devastating. J. B. Phillips has shown in *Is God at Home?* how even words as familiar as the Beatitudes challenge the very roots of our daily attitudes and assumptions. Most people think:—

> Blessed are the 'pushers': for they get on in the world.
> Blessed are the hard-boiled: for they never let life hurt them.
> Blessed are they who complain: for they get their own way in the end.
> Blessed are the blasé: for they never worry over their sins.

Blessed are the slave-drivers: for they get results.

Blessed are the knowledgeable men of the world: for they know their way around.

Blessed are the trouble-makers: for they make people take notice of them.

But Jesus Christ said:

'Blessed are the poor in spirit, for theirs is the kingdom of heaven.

Blessed are those who mourn, for they shall be comforted.

Blessed are the meek, for they shall inherit the earth.

Blessed are those who hunger and thirst for righteousness, for they shall be satisfied.

Blessed are the merciful, for they shall obtain mercy.

Blessed are the pure in heart, for they shall see God.

Blessed are the peacemakers, for they shall be called sons of God.'[1]

It is hardly surprising that the comment of the crowds after teaching of that calibre is that Jesus taught with authority, and not like the clergy. He did not even revive the formula of the prophets of old, 'Thus says the Lord.' With immense simplicity he declared 'I say to you', and he calmly told his hearers that his teaching would endure for ever. So far he has proved right. There hasn't been a single ethical advance, not a single fresh moral insight, in the nineteen hundred years since he taught. It makes you think. Is it just the human attractiveness of Jesus that accounts for all this?

The divine nature of Jesus

We do not find it easy to swallow the suggestion that Jesus was anything more than a good man. We *ought* not to find it easy. Nevertheless, the evidence must be faced: and the evidence is very strong. Many of his contemporaries found it conclusive. Living with Jesus, watching Jesus, listening to

[1] Matthew 5 : 4–9.

43

Jesus, assessing Jesus for three years or so, convinced them that he was no mere man.

Contemporary testimony

They struggled for words in which to express their growing convictions. They called him 'Son of God', an ancient title used in the Old Testament for God's royal representative, the king of Israel. Each successive king proved more or less of a disappointment, and men of faith in Israel longed for the day when a king, as they put it, 'would reign in righteousness': when God's kingly rule should be worthily expressed in a personal viceregent. This, they came to believe, was precisely what Jesus was. He gave perfect embodiment to God's kingly rule, to the Creator's royal claims on human allegiance. Hence all the talk in the Gospels about the kingdom or kingly rule of God which Jesus brought in and which men could enter by following him.

Testimony by Jesus

The Gospels give us another highly significant title for Jesus; one which, curiously enough, is found only on his own lips as a self-designation. It is 'Son of man', a phrase with an ambiguous lilt to it. It could mean no more in the Aramaic of his day than an oblique reference to oneself; rather as the French use *l'on*. But it would also undoubtedly take the minds of some of his hearers back to the prophecy in Daniel where the Son of man, representing God's people ('the saints of the Most High'), comes with the clouds of heaven and 'to him was given dominion and glory and kingdom, that all peoples, nations, and languages should serve him; his dominion is an everlasting dominion . . . and his kingdom shall not be destroyed'.[2] That must have shaken them, coming from a Galilean peasant. Indeed, it was the claim that clinched the opposition of the official priesthood. When the high priest put to Jesus the crucial question, 'Are you the Christ (*i.e.*

[2] Daniel 7 : 13, 14, 18.

44

anointed ruler), the Son of the Blessed One?' his reply was, 'I am; and you will see the Son of man sitting at the right hand of Power, and coming with the clouds of heaven.' 'Blasphemy!' shouted the high priest.[3] And he was right . . . unless, incredible though it seemed, what Jesus was claiming was the truth.

Testimony in the Letter to the Hebrews

His followers came to believe it was the truth, and they expressed their conviction in no uncertain terms. They said that God who had spoken partially and gradually through a succession of prophets in the days of old had now revealed himself fully and decisively in the person of his Son – the one by whom he made the world and for whom he made it, the one who corresponds as exactly to the invisible heavenly Father as a wax impression to the die that made it, or as radiance to the sun that produced it. That is how the unknown writer of the Letter to the Hebrews begins his Epistle.

Testimony by Paul

Paul uses similar language. Writing to Colossian Christians who were toying with the idea of a variety of mediators between man and God, he makes this exclusive and far-reaching claim for Jesus: 'He is the visible representation of the God we cannot see. He holds the primacy over all created things. By him everything in heaven and earth was brought into being. The whole universe was made by him and for him. He exists before all things, and the whole universe has its principle of coherence in him.'[4]

Reflect on those breathtaking words. They were penned by one of the most passionate monotheists in Israel and one of her most theologically educated sons; a man who was utterly convinced that there was but one God, the Creator of heaven and earth, and that therefore no image of him

[3] Mark 14 : 61–64.
[4] Colossians 1 : 15ff.

was acceptable for one moment. Yet Saul of Tarsus had found himself compelled to gaze on Jesus; and in Jesus he saw the human face of God. In his own contemporary, a man from Nazareth, he saw the one who was the instrument in creation, the goal to which the whole world was tending, and the principle of coherence in the universe. Staggering! Yet he was convinced of it. He taught it. He suffered mockery and rejection for doing so; indeed, he willingly endured stoning, disenfranchisement, prison and death for proclaiming it without fear or favour.

He was not alone. A large and swiftly-growing company of colleagues made just the same claim and backed it up with similar privations. They were radiant in the conviction that God was no distant observer of the human scene, but that the Beyond had come into our midst, that the inscrutable divine Lord had taken our human nature on him, that Jesus was the window into God.

Testimony by John

John was just one of these contemporaries. He used one of the metaphysical terms common in moderately thoughtful circles in his day and called Jesus 'the Word'. Part of his meaning would run something like this. Just as my words enable you to grasp the otherwise inscrutable workings of my mind, so Jesus is God's Word, enabling you to grasp in terms intelligible to human beings the invisible God. 'In the beginning was the Word, and the Word was with God, and the Word was God . . . And the Word became flesh and dwelt among us, and we gazed on his glory, glory as of the only Son of the Father.'[5] He goes on to tremble on the brink of meaninglessness when he calls Jesus not the 'only begotten Son of God', which would have been shattering enough, but, as the oldest and most recently discovered mss show, 'the only begotten *God*, the one who has fully expounded what the Father is'.[6] And in his Epistle John

[5] John 1 : 1, 14.
[6] John 1 : 18.

46

begins in a similar vein, and adds in ringing tones the assertion that this is *real*. 'We have heard, we have looked upon, we have handled the Word of life . . . and we proclaim him to you.'[7] It takes God to reveal God.

The grounds of their belief

How were these Jewish monotheists convinced that Jesus was divine as well as human? It was the last thing they wanted to believe. It went against their upbringing, their religion, their reason. But they were convinced by the sheer weight of the evidence.

It is an interesting exercise to look through the New Testament records and see what it was that brought men and women to faith in Jesus.

Jesus' teaching

It was his teaching, for one thing. 'Never man spoke like this man!'[8] said some soldiers who had been sent to arrest him, when they returned, their task unaccomplished. And they were right. There has been no parallel in the history of the world to the quality, the content and the power of the teaching of Jesus. Nobody has been able to show any evil contained in it. Nobody has been able to show any good not contained in it. People were amazed at it: 'How does this man know so much, never having been to university?' Jesus' simple answer was to say: 'My teaching is not mine, but his that sent me. If any man is willing to do his will, he will have no doubts as to where the teaching comes from – whether from God or whether I speak from myself.'[9]

Jesus' character

This teaching was backed up by a flawless character. So flawless that, even when at his trial they put up false witnesses to arraign him, they could not agree in their

[7] 1 John 1 : 1.
[8] John 7 : 46.
[9] John 7 : 15ff.

47

testimony. So flawless that Pilate three times declared him innocent, and Pilate's wife had a nightmare about the judicial murder of this innocent man. So flawless that the centurion at the cross, hardened as he was to bloodshed, declared, 'This man was innocent.' So flawless that his friends – his friends, mark you – maintained that he was completely sinless: indeed, tough fisherman that he was, Simon Peter once fell at his feet and begged him to depart from a sinful person like himself. So flawless that, when faced by an angry crowd out for his blood, Jesus could calmly ask them, 'Which of you can point to something wrong that I have done?' – and get no reply. So flawless was his character that, unlike one of the great saints of any religion, who are always the first to recognize their own shortcomings, Jesus could say, 'I do always those things that please my heavenly Father.'[1] That is the man, that is the life from whom those matchless teachings came. It meant that when he quietly claimed to be the supreme self-disclosure of God to men, and the only way from men to the Father, they believed him.[2] 'Everything is entrusted to me by my Father; and no one knows the Son but the Father, and no one knows the Father but the Son, and those to whom the Son may choose to reveal him.' As if that were not enough, Jesus continued, 'Come to me, all whose work is hard, whose load is heavy . . . and learn from me.'[3] The Jews would have taken the point in a way that is hard for us to grasp. For to them divine Wisdom, enshrined in the Old Testament Scriptures, was the place to which they must turn for instruction.[4] Jesus, in other words, is claiming the place occupied by the words of God in Scripture. He sees his teaching as the crown of God's revelation through the Old Testament; and his life lent credibility to the claim.

---

[1] John 8 : 29.
[2] John 14 : 4–11.
[3] Matthew 11 : 27ff.
[4] See, *e.g.*, Proverbs 8 and 9. *Cf.* also Ecclesiasticus 51 : 23.

Jesus' miracles

They believed Jesus for another reason: his miracles. This is not a popular theme in today's society, which is sceptical about the miraculous and supremely confident in the laws of nature. But all down the centuries the miracles of Jesus have been a very strong plank in the Christian case. And rightly so. They were so undeniably a part of his impact, so closely integrated with his whole ministry, that it is impossible to find any strand in the tradition that is not shot through with the miraculous. The Jesus who meets us in the pages of the New Testament is unashamedly supernatural, and cannot be shrunk into a naturalistic figure fitting conveniently into our comfortable categories for religious teachers! For nearly a century men tried to shrink him, with their liberal *Lives of Jesus*. Since the work of Schweitzer and Barth at the beginning of this century, however, it has been recognized on all sides that this cannot be done. The fact is that the miracles were so much part of Jesus' self-disclosure that John chose seven of them, called them signs, and built his Gospel round them. By giving an account of each of them, together with an explanatory discourse, he shows us what Jesus' real significance is.

The miracles were so well attested that we find the opponents of Jesus unable to deny them, and forced to assign them to an evil power. 'Through the ruler of the demons he casts out the demons,' said the Pharisees. 'But how can the devil cast out the devil?' asked Jesus. 'In that case his control would come to an end' – which is manifestly not the case![5] The interesting thing to notice is that they did not, and could not, deny the efficacy of the cures. In later years they said that he had learnt magic in Egypt, and that he was crucified on the eve of Passover for having practised sorcery in Israel. That was the official party line. But so clear was the power of his miracles that we find Jewish people trying to make use of that power without yielding their lives to Jesus. In the Acts of the Apostles we find some

[5] Mark 3 : 22ff.

of these people attempting exorcism 'by the Jesus whom Paul proclaims'. With a touch of humour the writer recounts how the man with the evil spirit flew at them shouting 'Jesus I acknowledge, and I know about Paul, but who are you?', overpowered them all, and handled them so roughly that they ran out of the house stripped and battered![6] There are several prohibitions in later Jewish writings against healing in the name of Jesus: 'A man shall have no dealing with the heretics, nor be cured by them, even for the sake of an hour of life.'

But, you will say, however well attested the miracles of Jesus are, and however much others in antiquity wanted to emulate them, we simply can't credit them in this scientific age. And why not? If Jesus really was not just human, but God come to give us freedom, why should there not be some indication of the fact through the acts of power which he used? They are never for display, you will notice, and never for selfish purposes. They are either to heal or to show Christ's mastery over the elements, and thereby demonstrate some facet of who he is. It is certainly not scientific to reject such a claim out of hand. If one hundred years ago you had claimed you could talk to a man the other side of the Atlantic in America without a 'phone, or if fifty years ago you had claimed that man would go to the moon, it would have been declared scientifically impossible. Now it is commonplace. Laws of nature are not rigid, unalterable entities. They are merely the expressions of observed uniformities in the workings of nature. Well, by definition there is nothing comparable to the invasion of this earth by God in the first years of our era. No laws of nature, no question of observed uniformities, are involved. The truly scientific method for us is to examine the evidence and reflect on it.

That is what made believers of Jesus' contemporaries. Jesus turned the water into wine; and this, we read, 'led

[6] Acts 19 : 13ff.

his disciples to believe in him'.[7] The raising of Lazarus to life had the same effect: 'Many of the Jews who had come to visit Mary and had seen what Jesus did, put their faith in him.'[8] On one occasion Jesus was confronted by a crowd in the temple precincts who pressed him as to who he really was. 'I have told you,' said Jesus, 'but you do not believe. My deeds done in my Father's name are my credentials. . . . My Father and I are one.' This, understandably, did not go down very well, and they picked up stones to throw at him, but Jesus asked them, 'Do you charge me with blasphemy because I said, "I am God's Son"? If I am not acting as my Father would, do not believe me. But if I am, accept the evidence of my deeds, even if you do not believe me.'[9] The miraculous actions of Jesus did bear testimony to his person as Son of God. And many came to faith in him that way.

Jesus' fulfilment of Scripture

And then, of course, there was his fulfilment of Scripture. This again led many people to belief. The Old Testament was accepted as God's word to Israel. Yet, authoritative as it was, it was clearly incomplete. It looked for a coming deliverer of God's people not merely from external enemies but from self-will. This person was variously described in different strands of the Old Testament as the Son of God, the Son of man, the Suffering Servant of the Lord, the one of David's house filled with the Spirit of the Lord, and so on. This coming Saviour would forge a new covenant between God and his people which would be internal, personal, lasting, and involved the forgiveness of sins. He would act as a shepherd to God's scattered people. He would heal, and teach in parables, and be anointed by the Lord 'to preach good news to the poor, to bind up the broken-hearted, to proclaim liberation to the captives and the opening of

[7] John 2: 11.
[8] John 11: 45.
[9] John 10: 25, 30, 36-38.

51

prison to those who were bound, to announce the year of the Lord's good pleasure . . .'.[1] But the Scriptures went on to predict that this coming Deliverer would be despised and rejected, that the people he came to save would spurn him, that he would suffer and die. In his death he would be deemed accursed, and would be accompanied by criminals. His grave would belong to a rich man. And yet, somehow or other, this would not be the end. There are various hints of his resurrection, or at least his vindication by God after men have rejected him. 'Behold, my servant shall be exalted and lifted up, and shall be very high' and 'When he makes himself an offering for sin, he shall see his offspring, he shall prolong his days . . . he shall see the fruit of the travail of his soul and be satisfied. Through knowing him many shall be accounted right with God, and he shall bear their iniquities. Therefore I will divide him a portion with the great, and he shall divide the spoil with the strong.'[2]

Now we know from a collection of Messianic texts found in a cave at Qumran, that people were indeed looking for the coming great Deliverer and searching the Old Testament scriptures with anxious expectation during the fifty years or so before the birth of Jesus. Hardly surprising when Roman occupying troops were stumping all over what was supposed to be God's holy land. But nobody ever fitted these ancient prophecies – until Jesus. Despite their Teacher of Righteousness, whom they greatly respected, the men of Qumran were still looking forward to the arrival of a priestly ruler, a royal ruler, and a prophet like Moses. Eventually, unknown to them, he actually came, from a little village called Bethlehem, and fulfilled all three roles. His very birth fitted in with those Old Testament prophecies: 'But from you, Bethlehem, shall come forth for me one who is to be ruler in Israel, whose origin is from of old. . . . Then the rest of his brethren shall return to the people of Israel. And he shall stand and feed his flock in the

[1] Isaiah 61 : 1f.
[2] Isaiah 52 : 13 – 53 : 12.

strength of the Lord, in the majesty of the name of the Lord his God.'[3] That is just what he did.

There's a great deal more that could be said about this theme of fulfilling the Scriptures. And it is no good saying that he rigged the circumstances of his life so as to appear to fulfil them – for the simple truth is that most of them concern his birth and death, and these are two areas where 'rigging' can't be done. Accordingly, we read 'and they believed the scripture . . . ', 'and the scripture was fulfilled . . . ', 'as yet the scripture had not dawned on them that he must rise from the dead . . . ', 'and beginning with Moses and all the prophets Jesus interpreted to them (*i.e.* the two disciples walking to Emmaus after the resurrection) the things concerning himself'.[4] These are typical New Testament descriptions of the impact made on the contemporaries of Jesus by the way his birth, life and death all fitted in with the ancient prophecies. Indeed, many of the distinguished converts to Christianity in the second century seem to have come to belief through reading the Scriptures and seeing that Christ was in fact the fulfilment. I remember on two occasions, when seeking to help Jewish people to faith in Christ, adopting just this method of using the ancient prophecies of the Old Testament, and seeing the light of understanding dawn in their eyes as they began to recognize and trust the one who fulfilled them.

There were three other reasons why these Jewish monotheists came to the scandalous conviction that Jesus was divine.

The cross of Jesus
One was the manner of his death. Jesus had said that, if lifted up from the earth, he would draw all types of person to himself, and this has proved abundantly true. Until the cross of Christ the faith of the disciples was weak and

[3] Micah 5 : 1–4.
[4] John 2 : 22; Mark 15 : 28; John 20 : 9; Luke 24 : 27.

53

incoherent. The cross which you might have thought would have crushed such faith as they had, in fact lit it into an inextinguishable blaze. And that is a very remarkable thing. Remarkable to start believing in your leader once he is dead and gone. Remarkable to start believing that he is God's anointed rescuer once he has so signally failed to produce any political settlement of the Roman problem and has in fact been executed by them as a pretender to power – who failed. Most remarkable of all when you recall that in the Old Testament it says that anyone exposed on a cross must be seen as resting under the curse of God.[5] Remarkable, but true. The Christian movement only began to catch light once Jesus was crucified. The cross became the symbol of the new movement. The symbol of death and shame turned into the most glorious badge of discipleship. How did it happen?

It was, I think, as they saw him die that understanding began to dawn. The sheer self-sacrifice of it; the gentleness, the unselfishness, the love, the victory of it made them wonder, made them perceive. Listen to Peter, who was there. He is writing years later about Christian submissiveness in the face of provocation. 'For to this you have been called, because Christ also suffered for you, leaving you an example, that you should follow in his steps. He committed no sin; no guile was found on his lips. When he was reviled, he did not revile in return; when he suffered, he did not threaten; but he trusted to him who judges justly.'[6] Yes, Peter seems to say, that is the pattern for the Christian free man. That is how Jesus, the free man's model, behaved at the supreme crisis of his life; though apparently defeated, he was conqueror in that situation by the very way he handled it. But Peter cannot stop there. Seeing Jesus die with such self-control, such love for others that he prayed for his executioners, thought about his mother's future welfare whilst on the cross, and accepted

[5] Deuteronomy 21 : 22f.
[6] 1 Peter 2 : 21ff.

54

the homage of a dying thief executed next to him – why, this showed Peter what was really happening on that first Good Friday. He continues: 'He himself bore our sins in his own body on that tree' and 'tree' is the name the Old Testament gives for the place on which a man is accursed if he hangs there. It is plain that Peter has begun to see that although Jesus died in the place of cursing, the curse was not his, but ours. He did indeed bear sins; but they were our sins, not his own, for he had none. 'By his wounds you have been healed,' he concludes, quoting from Isaiah 53, the chapter that foretells the death of the sacrificial, sin-bearing, Suffering Servant of the Lord.[7]

It is perfectly astounding that through the squalid murder of Calvary his followers should have received such lasting assurance about who Jesus was. But such is undeniably the case. Mark, in his account, tells of the death of Jesus and immediately goes on: 'And the temple curtain was ripped in half from the top to the bottom.' That curtain hung there to remind everybody to keep out of the inner sanctuary, the place where God's presence was located. But when the curtain was torn to pieces like that, it was the indication that the way into God's presence was opened up for anyone to go in. And in his very next words, Mark hints at the Gentiles entering in through that curtain, so to speak (thousands had already done so by the time he wrote his Gospel in the 60s of the first century), for the centurion in charge of the execution squad makes the distinctively Christian assertion, 'Truly this man was the Son of God.'[8] John, for his part, stresses the victory of Jesus in the cross. This was no inescapable doom: Jesus went freely to his death. He was utterly in control of the whole situation. This was no defeat: it was triumph, triumph over all the forces of evil arrayed against him, and it culminates in the shout 'Finished': the task is done.[9] Paul, too, came to see in

[7] 1 Peter 2 : 24f.
[8] Mark 15 : 38f.
[9] John 19 : 30.

the cross the very heart of what Jesus was and had done for men. 'God was in Christ reconciling the world to himself, not counting their wrongdoings against them,' or, when he is quoting the early creed which he learnt at the beginning of his Christian life in the 30s, 'Christ died for our sins according to the scriptures.'[1]

The resurrection of Jesus

But even the cross would scarcely have had this lasting effect upon his contemporaries without the resurrection. They were not easily convinced. It required solid, palpable evidence that Jesus was alive again after three days in the tomb to bring Thomas to belief. 'Unless I see in his hands the print of the nails, and place my finger in the mark of the nails, and place my hand in his side, I will not believe.' That was his ultimatum. And Jesus graciously met it. 'He said to Thomas, "Put your finger here, and see my hands; and put out your hand, and place it in my side; do not be faithless, but believing." Thomas answered him, "My Lord and my God!"'[2]

It was the resurrection that brought Thomas to faith. It did the same for Peter. He wrote: 'Born again to a living hope through the resurrection of Christ from the dead.'[3] The same was true of Paul. It was when he met face to face with the risen Christ on the Damascus road that he changed from persecutor into believer.[4] So did James. James was a member of Jesus' family – yet he did not believe in him during his ministry. Indeed, he subscribed to the family view that Jesus was a fanatic.[5] But we find that he became the leader of the church in Jerusalem only a few short years after the crucifixion. The reason? He had met with Jesus after the resurrection. 'He appeared', we read,

[1] 2 Corinthians 5 : 19; 1 Corinthians 15 : 4.
[2] John 20 : 25–28.
[3] 1 Peter 1 : 3.
[4] 1 Corinthians 15 : 8, 9.
[5] John 7 : 5; Mark 3 : 21.

'to James.'[6] Just that. No more. But it speaks volumes. It was that interview with the risen Jesus that turned James from critic to Christian.

Their experience of Jesus
Those were the facts which brought the people who were there to the belief that Jesus was God no less than man. They are good reasons. They still hold water. But there was one more. They believed because of their experience. Jesus had said, for example, 'I am the bread of life; he who comes to me shall never hunger, and he who believes in me shall never thirst.'[7] They had believed in him, and they had found it was true that he satisfied them as he had promised. This accounts for the note of discovery, of assurance, of joy that radiates out through the books of the New Testament. These men had found treasure, and they were determined to share it. How could they keep quiet? They had lived alongside the one who made sense of everything in the world, the free man's model, the key that unlocked the nature of reality. They had something to shout about. For they had begun by being intrigued by the human attractiveness and had gone on to be convinced by the divine nature of Jesus. They were like men born all over again. And this leads on to the third strand about the real Jesus that runs right through the New Testament evidence.

The liberating power of Jesus

Quite literally, Jesus spells freedom. The word means 'God to the rescue'.[8] And that is what the early disciples found him to be. And, fortunately, it need not stop there. The risen presence of Christ in the life remains the most liberating force in the world.

[6] 1 Corinthians 15 : 7.
[7] John 6 : 35.
[8] Matthew 1 : 21.

57

Release from guilt

Jesus spells freedom from guilt. One of the most notable emphases in the Acts of the Apostles is the repeated offer, 'Through this man forgiveness of sins is proclaimed to you.'[9] That is a commodity that cannot be procured anywhere else in the world, and therefore we soft-pedal the disease for which it is the remedy. But human wickedness lies at the root of almost all our troubles. And when Jesus takes a man in hand he erases the ugly stains of the past, for the simple but gloriously conclusive reason that he took our place and died our death on the cross. Freedom from guilt! You might be a civilized sinner like Saul of Tarsus: but when he compared himself with what he ought to be, Saul came to see himself as 'the chief of sinners' and cried out in gratitude for 'release through his death'.[1] You might be a crude sinner like many of the Corinthians, of whom we read that they had been 'idolaters, adulterers, homosexuals, thieves, drunkards . . . But you were washed, you were sanctified, you were justified in the name of the Lord Jesus Christ and in the Spirit of our God'.[2] Whether I am a socially acceptable sinner or flagrantly immoral makes little difference. I become a new man once I know that I am set free from that accusing finger, that ever-growing load of past wrongdoing.

Here is a respectable sinner finding the liberation Christ can give: 'It is a wonderful thing to discover God, to unplug your ears and hear him, to open your eyes and see him, especially at five minutes after midnight! But it has happened. I suppose I have been, I mean I am, a sinner, with offences against God and against myself, but I can feel so much lighter in my brain, knowing that there is a love to absolve my sins, knowing that there is repentance.'

That letter came to me out of the blue from a teenage girl. Very different was Bill, the ex-gangster I met recently.

[9] *E.g.* Acts 13 : 38.
[1] 1 Timothy 1 : 15; Ephesians 1 : 7.
[2] 1 Corinthians 6 : 9–11.

58

He had been head of a crime syndicate of armed robbers, and had been sentenced to 29 years in prison. Twice he engineered escapes from top-security wings. This man was converted in prison, and during his last three years there his life was exemplary. Since release, after serving fourteen years of his term, he has gone back on occasion to bear testimony to Christ among his old prisoner colleagues, and is not only going straight but is reconciled with his wife and family and is actively engaged in Christian work. Christ has liberated him from the past.

He has done the same for Roy, a young man who was in and out of Borstal and prison for years. After a beating one day, he was lying on the cell floor, helpless and weak. 'In three words', he writes, 'I prayed a feeble unbelieving prayer: "God help me." But he answered, and through the chaplain I came face to face with the love of Christ. I asked him to be my Saviour. I realized that although a term of imprisonment could clear my debt to society, it took a personal "sorry" to God and also his forgiveness to keep me completely clean. God did for me what no prison could ever do. He forgave me for Christ's sake; and then he reformed me.' God did indeed, and that man is now training for the Anglican ministry at the College where I work.

Freedom from habit

Jesus spells freedom from bondage. The bondage to bad habit which we excuse by saying 'You can't change human nature'. Maybe you can't, but Christ can. Simon Peter found this with his impetuous nature, as we see it in the Gospels. How did he become the man of rock that we find in the Acts and Epistles? He gives us the answer in his own words: 'You are being kept by the power of God as you trust him for salvation.'[3] Paul had exactly the same experience. 'I can do anything through him who gives me power,'[4] he said. 'The law of the Spirit of life in Christ

[3] 1 Peter 1 : 5.
[4] Philippians 4 : 13.

Jesus has set me free from the law of sin and death.'[5] By this he meant that a higher principle than that of evil, none other than the Spirit of the risen Christ, had come to live in him and this accounted for his liberation from the habits that had once got him down.

I met a young man recently who had been a Christian, I discovered, for ten months. During that time he had led more people to Jesus Christ than he could remember, such was his vitality, his sense of discovery, fulfilment and mission. You can tell his background from the fact that he was high on opium and stoned on drink the night he heard about Jesus. He immediately became stone-cold sober, to his utter amazement. He put his faith in Christ that night, and Christ has changed his life triumphantly. There is power in Jesus Christ: he spells freedom.

Deliverance from fear

Our society is riddled with fear. Fear of the bomb, fear of what others will think, fear that our good looks will fade, fear that the job will fold up, fear of death. Jesus Christ liberates from fear. He turned those cowardly disciples who deserted him at his arrest into heroes who defied arrest, imprisonment, torture and death in his cause. He enabled Paul and Silas to sing praises in prison at midnight after an unjust beating. Simon Peter had learned the hard way to 'cast all your worries upon him', as he advised his Christian readers, 'for it matters to him about you'.[6] He certainly had assimilated the lesson. On the night before his execution we find him sleeping peacefully between his guards. He could have echoed the words written in identical circumstances by the Christian martyr Dietrich Bonhoeffer in 1944. He wrote to a friend: 'Please don't ever get anxious or worried about me, but don't forget to pray for me – I'm sure you don't! I am so sure of God's guiding hand, and I hope I shall never lose that certainty. You must never doubt that I

[5] Romans 8 : 2.
[6] 1 Peter 5 : 7.

am travelling my appointed road with gratitude and cheerfulness.' The peace of God may pass all human understanding, but mercifully not all human experiencing. It does mount guard over our feelings and our thinking processes as we ask Christ to take charge of the situation – just as Paul said it would. Freedom from anxiety, based on trust in the Son of God who loved me and gave himself for me, is a dimension of freedom that is beyond value.

The answer to loneliness

Jesus spells freedom from loneliness. 'Why am I so lonely when there are over 2,000 people here?' was found scratched on a student's desk. And we all know what it is to be lonely at a party, in a crowd or in a foreign land. Even the best of friends cannot assuage the terrible loneliness we experience at times. The early Christians discovered that Jesus brought wonderful liberation here. They heard his promise, 'I am with you always, right through to the end of the world';[7] they believed it, and they found it true. 'Be content with what you have,' wrote one early Christian; 'for he has said, "I will never fail you nor forsake you." Hence we can confidently say,

> "The Lord is my helper,
> I will not be afraid;
> what can man do to me?" '[8]

One of the most profound teachings in the New Testament is that God does not inhabit temples but people, the people who are willing to share their lives with him.[9] And he has pledged himself never to leave them in the lurch. Up till death and beyond, he is with us. Back to Bonhoeffer: 'We must always live close to the presence of God, for that is newness of life . . . no earthly power can touch us without his will, and danger can only drive us closer to him.' His

[7] Matthew 28 : 20.
[8] Hebrews 13 : 5, 6.
[9] 1 Corinthians 3 : 16.

experience, nineteen hundred years later, matched that of the apostle Paul. Listen to his rhetorical query: 'What can separate us from the love of Christ? Can affliction or hardship? Can persecution, hunger, nakedness, peril, or the sword?'[1] There spoke the man who, like Bonhoeffer, had known all these things. And throughout them he knew the presence and the love of Christ.

Something to live for

Finally (for one must call a halt somewhere!), Jesus spells freedom from aimlessness. Had he merely been a religious teacher, his followers would have drifted back to their fishing and looked back in nostalgia. There is some evidence that this is precisely what they did immediately after his crucifixion. But when once the truth of the resurrection gripped them, they were immediately liberated from aimlessness. They now had a supremely important purpose for living. They were the commissioned representatives of Jesus. They were out to be of service to him who had freed them, by serving others for his sake. They did not see themselves as freed in order to be self-centred, but freed from self-centredness in order to be of use to God and man.

Quite recently the actor James Fox, who starred, for example, in *The Magnificent Men in their Flying Machines*, discovered Jesus Christ for himself. He found in Christ a satisfaction and direction for living such as he had never known before. He writes: 'To me the new life in Christ is one that is motivated and redirected by God to do his will. He shows me that will of his in the Bible and he enables me to understand it by his Holy Spirit. For the first time I have found a full and satisfying life, at peace with God and with people, by having the Holy Spirit as my comforter, teacher and guide into all the truth. I have been greatly helped recently by Paul's words in 2 Corinthians 4:16, "No wonder we do not lose heart! Though our outward humanity is in decay, yet day by day we are inwardly renewed." '

[1] Romans 8 : 35.

James Fox has found something to live for, something more satisfying and certainly more lasting than being a celebrity.

Christian freedom does not mean you can do your own thing, but God's thing, and his thing will involve self-giving for others (for that is his nature). It proves utterly satisfying for the simple reason that it is what we were made for. This is how the most human being who ever lived found his freedom. He lived his life in grateful dependence on the Father who designed and gave it. His service really is perfect freedom, as the old Prayer Book has it, because it is a glad and willing acceptance of our true nature and our ultimate purpose in the world.

The real Jesus, human, divine, contemporary, spells freedom.

3 Free love

LOVE IS man's deepest concern. Love brings us closest to reality. On that we are all agreed, Christian and atheist, young and old. But wait! Is there not some sleight of hand here? Surely Christians aren't keen on love, full-blooded, sexual love?

> 'You have stolen my heart, my sister,
>   you have stolen it, my bride,
>   with one of your eyes, with one jewel of your necklace.
> How beautiful are your breasts, my sister, my bride!
>   Your love is more fragrant than wine,
>   and your perfumes sweeter than any spices . . .
> I am my beloved's, and my beloved is mine . . .
> Wear me as a seal upon your heart,
>   as a seal upon your arm;
> for love is strong as death,
> passion fiercer than any flame.
> Many waters cannot quench love,
>   no flood can sweep it away;
> if a man were to offer for love
>   the whole wealth of his house,
>   it would be utterly scorned.'[1]

That comes from the Bible! Contrary to commonly-held prejudice, Christianity is not against sex. Christians revel in it as one of God's best gifts, both in itself, and as the prism

[1] Song of Solomon 4 : 9, 10; 6 : 3; 8 : 6, 7.

in which we catch a glimpse of his nature.

But just because Christians believe love is an aspect of God's nature and a gift of God's generosity, we dare to maintain a most unpopular thesis. We believe that full sexual love should be enjoyed in marriage or not at all. On one occasion Jesus was asked whether divorce was lawful or not. In reply he reminded his hearers of the ancient words of Genesis, that in the beginning God made them male and female. 'For this reason a man shall leave his father and mother, and be made one with his wife; and the two shall become one flesh.' 'What therefore God has joined together, let no man put asunder.'[2] In so doing he was pointing to the ideal for human partnership – a total self-giving to one partner for life. And sex is meant to be the means of expressing that love and deepening it.

Of course, if you are an atheist this point of view will not impress you. You believe there is no personal source to our being, that human nature is the chance product of impersonal factors, that human values have no ultimate validity. How can they? 'The world is absurd, nauseating,' say the existentialists who have so shaped modern attitudes. 'All the same, we must exercise our freedom in making the most of our situation. Love is both pleasant and personal, and enables us to escape for a while from the impersonal and the unpleasant. So on with love!'

If he were consistent the atheist should see love as no more than the expression of animal lust, of biological necessity. But I do not often find an atheist as consistent as this. Most seem to hold that love is some sort of an absolute; that love is real, that love brings you into touch with the nature of things. Could it be, after all, that love *is* real, love *is* part of the nature of things? Could it be an identification tag left by God in the hearts of those who have written him off in their rational being? Does he whisper as they fall in love, 'There is something beyond the purely animal and the material in love. It cannot be analysed in your test tube or

[2] Matthew 19 : 4f.

proved by your logic, but it is real'?

Be that as it may, atheist and Christian alike confess the supreme importance of love, though the Christian can add the rider, 'Love takes me to the heart of reality, for God is love. He invented it.' And if all are agreed that love is a good thing, then why not 'the more of it the merrier'? Why not free love all round?

Love that enslaves – Free sex

The answer is that random sex is self-destructive. The Russians discovered this shortly after the Revolution and since they saw what it did in the nineteen twenties they have checked it very sharply. As Professor Unwin observed in his *Sex and Culture*, every generation is free to choose between creative expression and sexual licence. The Russians have learnt that lesson. Not so the West. Perhaps we could learn from Nabokov's *Lolita*, which is not just a dirty book, but a profound analysis of our society, obsessed as it is with sexuality.

It is a simple story and a tragic one. The central figure, Humbert, is, perhaps significantly, a Russian *émigré*. All through his life he is haunted by a perverted lust for immature girls. As an adult he emigrates again, from France to the USA, the 'type-country' of the twentieth century. He hopes to find there, in that land of unlimited opportunity, the freedom to indulge his longings.

The whole book seems to utter this ironic recipe, 'Go West, if you want freedom and a future.' But it proves a mocking recipe, for he never finds freedom from his obsession, only a deepening bondage to it.

In America he gets a room in the house of a dull suburban widow. She has a daughter of twelve, Lolita. The mother falls in love with Humbert. He falls in love with Lolita, an unattractive urchin, spoilt, precocious, sexy and devoted to candy floss and comics. Humbert manages to resist his urges, even though opportunity offers. Instead he writes them in his diary. In order to keep near the girl who excites and tortures him, he unwillingly marries the widow. One day the inevitable happens. She discovers the diary. She is appalled by his depravity, writes a furious denunciation of him to her lawyer, runs out to post it – and is run over in the street, and killed.

With commendable presence of mind Humbert recovers and suppresses the letter. He is now the legal guardian of Lolita, his step-daughter. Even so, he does not seduce her. Instead the little innocent seduces him. Off they go in an old car, heading West for the wide-open prairies. Freedom beckons at last! The journey is a nightmare. Sage brush desert succeeds dry plain. They sink deeper and deeper into disillusionment and misery. He ends up insane in the condemned cell after committing a sex murder, whilst Lolita lives (apart from the time in bed) on trashy magazines, coke and endless pop records. She ends up pregnant, worn out before reaching adulthood, and married to a young engineer whose manhood has been shot away in the war. We leave them in an industrial slum.

This is a terrifying indictment of our society and our values. Europe, like Humbert, was once civilized and is now middle-aged, effete, obsessed with sex, and lost. The great American dream of new frontiers and wide horizons leading to unlimited opportunity and total freedom has petered out in a wilderness of motels, sex, boredom and infantile promiscuity. The great adventure of Western civilization has brought us on a fool's errand through nothing more fertile than sage brush desert and dry plain, to deposit us in a dreary little township, or to a shack in an industrial slum. Abandoning God and the traditional virtues, we follow a mirage of freedom into the wilderness littered with concrete and chromium-plated motels from which there is no escape except through fantasy, insanity and death.

Nabokov is not alone in his nightmare. He is only one of the modern writers who are fascinated by the current depersonalization of sex, the spiritual vacuum of today's world. Free love, they have seen very acutely, is seldom free . . . and seldom love.

Sex before marriage – Four questions

Ah, you say, but it's different with me. I mean to keep one bird for life – but it's foolish to wait for sex till we're married. Surely if I really love her, it is all right?

This is your decision, your life. But, if you are maintaining that premarital intercourse is the fruit of the highest, deepest love you are capable of, then I would like to ask a few questions.

1. Does love rob?

Robert Garrard tells of an occasion when he was in a coffee house with a horde of young people. The lights were dimmed, the music seductive. Next to him was a bearded character with his girl on his knee. 'You don't think we have to wait till we're married to have sex, do you?' he said. 'See that handbag?' said Garrard. 'Well, pick it up and take it home.' 'No, that would be stealing,' was the rejoinder from the bearded one. 'But you are suggesting,' went on Garrard, 'that it is wrong to take from a girl something that, if you later change your mind, you can restore, but perfectly OK to take from her what, if you change your mind, you can never restore, as you could that handbag.' Not merely her virginity, but the chance of coming to marriage fresh rather than second-hand. Partners who insist on sex before marriage in fact rob each other and themselves. They grasp clumsily at an experience which they always wanted, in their heart of hearts, to be much more than a passing pleasure. A symbol of tenderness, of control, of permanence. And they have lost that through their sexual greed.

2. Does love stop?

Of course not. But these affairs do. They are very passionate. They are often very short lived. There is much talk beforehand of endless love, devotion and self-sacrifice. But afterwards all that is left behind is so often just a tangle of disillusionment, tears, depression and self-reproach. A secretary friend of mine tells me of some of her former flat-mates in London. It was a story of free sex, abortion, broken hearts, the lot. She reckons that she has been in no sense the loser by waiting until marriage for sexual relationship. In stark contrast, one of her flat-mates went to bed with a man the second time she went out with him. He turned her out of bed the moment it was over and did not want to see her again. She went home heartbroken. Sex has become a thing, and the person merely the occasion. What a revealing incident it is in George Orwell's *1984*, when the anti-hero, before going to bed with his girl, demands a reassurance. 'You like doing this? I don't mean simply me: I mean the thing itself.' He is not satisfied until he gets the answer, 'I adore it!' Preoccupation with the thing itself ousts consideration for the beloved. The other person merely becomes a sort of thrill-making machine, and the whole relationship is depersonalized. Sensory pleasure is the goal, and the partner can be and often is discarded as quickly as the cigarette packet once the cigarettes have been smoked.

3. Does love hurt?

If you love someone, will you expose them to hurt? Yet there is hurt in plenty when sex outside marriage is in question. Abortion soars. VD soars. Illegitimacy soars, despite contraception. So much so, in fact, that in the last fifteen years, legitimate births have gone up by 20% and illegitimate by 100%. The wife of one of the students at our College worked in a home for unmarried mothers. She told me once, 'I wish I could get hold of the men who messed about with these girls for pleasure. I'd like to show

69

them the misery that has resulted.' Does love hurt?

Even if contraception were perfect, you would leave your loved one to live with fear. Does love do that? 'Real love casts out fear,' so the New Testament says, 'and fear has torment.'[3] The torment of the girl who fears she is doing wrong; who fears her parents might find out; who fears month after month that she may be pregnant; who fears that it may not last.

4. Is love selfish?

To isolate and indulge your animal instincts at the expense of other values is selfish, even if both of you want it. It is selfish to remove sex from its proper context of children and companionship: the three of them should form a triangle of love. It is selfish to indulge your desires because you have not got the moral fibre to resist. The person who unwraps his present before Christmas Day is not the gainer but the loser. Among other things he loses self-respect. I have never met a sex-before-marriage man who honestly gained in self-respect. Have you?

Trust is such an important part of marriage. If before marriage a couple show that they can't control their sexual impulses, what sort of a basis is that for building the relationship of happy marriage – which necessitates confidence, respect, trust and self-sacrifice? Nothing shows more clearly than premarital sex the essentially selfish nature of man. I want, so I must have. Live now – pay (if necessary) later. It is all so selfish.

A love that robs, that hurts, that stops and is selfish is scarcely worthy of the name of love at all. That it should go by the name of 'free love' is the height of irony.

And yet, our frail gropings after true love give us an inkling of something very wonderful. A love that is personal and lasting, satisfying and ennobling, unselfish and sacrificial. That is what we dream about, even though we don't achieve it. Our loves fall short in various ways. They

[3] 1 John 4 : 18.

are mixed with selfishness, pleasure-seeking, greed and thoughtlessness. We have some conception of the ideal, but somehow it eludes our grasp. Is there an answer?

Love that liberates – Five aspects

Christianity declares that there is an answer. It declares that our instinct that love is the most important thing in the world is a right instinct. It says that God is love,[4] and that in his love we see the ideal of which our own affections give us a glimpse. Christianity does not say that love is God, that love is king, that so long as love is present nothing else matters. No. God is love. And 'God is love' suggests to me that it ought to be possible to look at human love and gain some clue as to what his love is like. After all, in his love he made us, and made us in some sense like himself. I want to suggest that there are at least five elements in all love that is real and free, elements which are supremely true of the love of God.

1. Love implies persons
That is almost too obvious to mention, but it is important and often forgotten. We can't love an object or an idea or a robot – not in the deep, full sense of love. Love implies persons. The same holds good with God. The New Testament is full of the astounding assertion that God loves the world, that God loves us, that God loves me. And as love is only possible between persons, that means that God is at least personal. No doubt he is, as C. S. Lewis's famous book pointed out, 'beyond personality'. But he is not less personal than the people he has created. And that is quite enough for me. Although I cannot hope to understand more than a tiny fraction of the divine Lover, I am assured that he is not totally unlike me; for he loves. What an encouragement to think that we derive not from some cold

[4] 1 John 4 : 8.

First Cause or disinterested Cosmic Architect, but from Love.

'Oh,' you say, 'there you go again, dragging God into it. I can't believe in God. It's irrational.' Irrational? What nonsense! You can't prove the existence of God, to be sure. But, as we have already seen in chapter 1, you can't prove any sort of personal existence. The appropriate way to assure yourself of the reality of persons is to meet them, not to try to prove them! No, proof is not appropriate: but don't tell me there is no evidence.

There is the evidence of the world, first of all. It must come from chance or a Creator. If chance, how is it that causation is built into every structure of it? How do you get a complicated link of cause and effect (upon which, as an axiom, all scientific method depends) if the whole world comes from chance? Can you pretend that is probable?

Then there is the evidence of design in this world of ours. My son is getting a microscope for Christmas this year. He will, I have no doubt, do his best to examine the symmetry of a snowflake, if he can catch it before it melts! Is there no design there? None in the radar equipment of a bat? None in the fact that bees visit flowers only during the limited hours in the day when they produce nectar? Wherever you look in nature, you find evidence of design. By all means say it all happened by chance. But don't expect me to believe that is the natural or rational explanation.

There is the evidence provided by human personality. Try as we will, we cannot persuade ourselves that human nature is junk. People are not just things. But how do you get personality if the universe has nothing but the impersonal behind it? Can it be that the river has risen higher than its source? Possible, doubtless, but not the natural explanation. Like begets like. And if I find human personality in the world, I would naturally postulate a personal Creator – unless I had a particular axe to grind in maintaining an atheist position.

Then there is the evidence of values. Are moral values,

are truth, beauty, goodness, freedom, love merely human impositions on an essentially meaningless world? Or do they, as most people feel deep down in their bones, have some validity in themselves? If so, what are they doing in a world that had no Creator, no Intelligence, no Moral Source, no Destiny?

Fifthly, there is the evidence provided by conscience. 'I ought' does not mean the same as 'It will pay me', nor 'this is how society wants me to behave'. To suppose it does is a complete category confusion. Indeed most of the moral advances in the world have been brought about by courageous men following their consciences when it assuredly did not pay them and when society all round them was most unwelcoming to the change. Think of the classic example of the abolition of slavery. Now what I want to know is, how do you find moral absolutes knocking around in a Godless, purposeless world? My guess is that Someone who is concerned about right and wrong, because he is a moral being, implanted in us that recognition of right and wrong. But I could be wrong. It may be an inherent quality in plankton!

Sixthly, there is the evidence provided by religion. Wherever you go in the world, from the most sophisticated countries to the most aboriginal, men worship God. Even in animistic or polytheistic cultures you generally find there is an archetypal god behind all the others in the pantheon. Even in professedly atheist countries such as Russia and Yugoslavia you find the Christian faith growing the more luxuriantly for being discouraged or actively repressed. Atheist régimes themselves have God-substitutes in place of the Almighty. Take the idolatry accorded to Mao, or to Lenin, and you will see what I mean. A friend told me recently of his latest visit to Russia. In Red Square he watched a woman lead a big party of schoolchildren to the plinth of Lenin. There they knelt and addressed the statue. They promised that they would obey Lenin's commands. Then they stood and raised their hands in silent salute.

Worship indeed! If not God, then a god-substitute. Now, tell me, whence did that instinct for worship arise in a universe that had no Creator? An odd thing to have evolved in the human animal, isn't it? And even odder that we have not been able to erase it, if it were just an ancient survival with no practical value, like the appendix.

The seventh piece of evidence we have considered in the last chapter. It is Jesus Christ. All the other pieces of evidence you can explain away, if you try hard enough. They do not and cannot prove God. Because, as we have seen, you don't prove people. You meet them. That is why the New Testament never tries to prove God's existence. It says, instead, 'Take a long look at Jesus. That is where you can meet God. That is where you can see that he is personal. That is where you can see he is love.'

2. Love requires honesty

It doesn't get far without it. That is why the history of romantic love is studded with lovers' quarrels. Love must be ruthlessly honest with the beloved. No pretence can stand before love. It must be real. Quite often people in love tell me of quarrels between them, and wonder whether they ought to marry in view of them. Frankly, I am encouraged when I hear them talk this way. They are dissatisfied with any pretence. They are impatient with unlovely traits of character in each other and want to get them talked over and put right. That seems to me to be real love. Love is fire as well as sweetness. It burns up all impurities in the object of its love.

That is why it seems to me highly appropriate that the Bible should have so much to say about the holiness and the judgment of God. It is made very plain throughout the Old Testament as well as the New, that God is love, and that his passionate concern for us, the objects of his love, makes him intolerant of the impurities of life and unloveliness of character that spoil us. That's how love should be, isn't it? No pretence will do. We cannot deceive him, however much we may kid others that we are good fellows at heart. His eyes, the Bible tells us, are like a flame: our God is a consuming fire. There is nothing flaccid and soft about the love of God. It is full-blooded love, pure and holy. And as he looks at us he is not impressed. He sees the greed, the lust, the lying, the suspicion, the arrogance, the selfishness, the apathy that skulk there. His love does not pretend this is not the case. It does not cover up our sins, as though it were a blanket. It shows up our failures, as if it were a searchlight. You have only to compare your character with Christ's to see how substandard it is. And that matters to God. It hurts him. He cannot tolerate it in the ones he loves. And who can blame him? His love is the implacable enemy of all that is unworthy in us.

Look at the same thing, if you will, another way. God has lavished his love on us. Making us in the first place, caring for us all our lives, coming for us in Jesus. And what did men do to a love like that? They nailed it to a cross. They saw the Ideal, and they could not bear it. They had to drive it away.

Has human nature changed since those far-off days? Not significantly, I think. We still tell the love of God to go away. We snap our fingers at his mercy and discuss how improper it would be of him to allow anyone to go to hell. Of course he cannot *bear* us to go to hell, to be lost from his love for ever. That is why he came to this earth; that is why he went to the cross: to barricade the path to hell. But for men to refuse his mercy whilst taking his mercy for granted is the ultimate impertinence. If persisted in, it will spell final ruin. For God's love, like all true love, is ruthlessly honest.

3. Love doesn't give up

All lovers think that their love will be permanent. Sometimes it does not turn out that way. Hearts get broken. It is a horrible thing to get jilted. We may well wonder whether the heavenly lover will jilt the human race, appalled at what he finds there. D. H. Lawrence asked himself this question in *Women in Love*: What would happen if the human race ran into a cul-de-sac and expended itself? He answers, 'Either the heart would break, or cease to care. Best cease to care. The timeless creative mystery would bring forth some other being, finer, more wonderful: some new, more lovely race, to carry on the game.'

That is the best answer a sensitive agnostic can suppose: scrap the lot and start again. But that is not the way of the God of the Bible. He does not abandon the human race to its richly deserved fate. He does not cease to care, either, though his heart of love does break at the hardness of our hearts. Instead he shows us a third alternative: a love that doesn't give up. That love came for us. That love died for us. That love lives for us, awaiting our response. That love preserves us every day. It is on this basis of achievement that he asks us to believe him when he promises to believers, 'I have loved you with an everlasting love',[5] and 'I will never leave you nor forsake you'.[6]

Nothing in all creation can separate a Christian from his Lord's enduring love. And to be assured of that love in every circumstance of life, in toil and loneliness, in pain and bereavement, in leadership and responsibility – why, this is freedom indeed! This permanent love of God offers me a relationship of trust in which I can grow as a person; a relationship of belonging which links me with all other Christians; and a relationship of compassion which empowers me to love the unlovely and care for them. It is the presence of this permanent, understanding love of God that both makes the Christian home so attractive and also drives Christians out the world over to give themselves for the alcoholic and the tramp, the head-hunter and the diseased. Where do they get the dynamic for this demanding life of love from? Quite simply, from the love of God to them, a love which endures.

[5] Jeremiah 31 : 3.
[6] Hebrews 13 : 5.

4. Love makes sacrifices

We have almost lost, in modern speech, the flavour of that word 'sacrifice' which meant so much to ancient man. We don't use it any more except in religious language, which almost nobody understands. But we do use it in connection with love. Because we very well know that all true love evokes sacrifice. If you love someone you'll do things for them – costly things, difficult things, menial things. Love is like that. Unselfish.

So much that passes for love today is not unselfish. It is, in fact, lust masquerading as love, and that is why it is so unsatisfactory. For lust says 'I', whilst love says 'You'. Lust says 'I must have', whilst love says 'I must give'. How quickly we appreciate this rare quality of unselfishness in the lover; but all too often we are disappointed. There is in erotic love a strong element that says 'I' rather than 'You', that grabs rather than gives. We aren't very good at understanding unselfish love.

Perhaps that is why the New Testament has to coin a new word for it. The Greeks had a perfectly good word for friendship, affection between equals. It was *philia*. They had a perfectly good word for erotic love, *erōs*. What the coming of Jesus did was to introduce a third word into the vocabulary of love, *agapē*. Unlike *philia*, whose philosophy is 'give that you may get', and unlike *erōs*, whose watchword is 'all get and no give', Jesus taught and embodied a quality of unselfish sacrificial love which was 'all give and no get'. God's love has no tinge of self-interest about it. It is pure self-giving.

The apostle John is the New Testament writer who seems to have reflected more deeply than any of the others on the nature of this love, though it is a major theme with them all. And John declares that God gives us a double demonstration of this *agapē*, this love of his. 'God is love,' he says; 'and his love was disclosed to us in this, that he sent his only Son into the world to bring us life.'[7] That's the first thing.

[7] 1 John 4 : 8, 9.

And it is very wonderful. When we think of a Sally Trench leaving her comfortable home and family to give herself in service to the meths drinkers; when we think of a brilliant doctor like Graham Scott-Brown giving up the prospect of following his father to Harley Street in order to go and serve the Nepalis in a mission hospital; when we think of a Schweitzer in the Congo forests or a Paul Brand among the lepers of India or a Helen Keller giving her life for the blind orphans of Jerusalem, then we get the message. That tells us something of what the love of God is like. He does not shrug his shoulders from a distance and say, 'They've got themselves into a mess: that's too bad.' He loves. So he comes in person, the person of Jesus, in order that we may share his life. That was costly for Trench and Schweitzer and Brand and the rest. Very costly. But it was *infinitely* costly for Jesus to come from his heavenly home to share our circumstances. Paul quotes a very early Christian hymn,[8] familiar to his readers at Philippi as they reflected on the sacrifice, the sheer unselfishness of that great stoop. 'For the divine nature was his from the first; yet he did not cling on to his equality with God, but made himself nothing, assuming the nature of a slave.' Think of that for a moment: the contrast between the divine nature, his from the first, and the nature of a slave, which he willingly took for us. The hymn continues: 'Bearing the human likeness, he humbled himself, and in obedience accepted even death – death on a cross.' Which brings us to the second and overwhelming proof of the supreme unselfishness of God's love for us, given us by the apostle John. 'I speak of the love he showed to us', he writes, 'in sending his Son as the remedy for the defilement of our sins.'[9]

We are impressed by self-sacrifice at any level. The patriot dying for his country, the captain going down with his ship after getting the women and children off first, the research doctor sacrificing his health for victims of disease. But

[8] Philippians 2 : 5–11.
[9] 1 John 4 : 10.

Jesus' death was no ordinary example of self-sacrifice. It did something. It changed things. It was the remedy for the defilement of our sins.

In the Bible there exists a very strong link between sin and death, between rebellion and estrangement, if you like. The point is made (it is a very elementary and obvious point, really, but we dislike it so much that we shut our eyes to the obvious) that if we choose to rebel against God then we get the alienation we have opted for.

What Jesus did on the cross was as man, representative man, proper man, to take the consequences of mankind's foolish and culpable rebellion. To 'bear sin', as the New Testament graphically describes it. That is to say, to take upon his own innocent shoulders the responsibility for the total human predicament. To take the consequences which human wickedness and folly had involved and exhaust them in his own person at the cost of his own life. He loved us enough to enter into our estrangement and death so as to make a way through to God, the source of reconciliation and life.

No human illustrations can possibly exhaust the meaning of the action. Increasingly I distrust using analogies to try to explain what he did there, and prefer to use the simple unadorned words of the New Testament itself. But perhaps these two military stories shed light on some aspects of the cross.

In the 1914–1918 war phone communications had broken down between headquarters and crucially important forward positions. Much depended on their speedy restoration, but the repair job was exceedingly dangerous, exposed as it was to concentrated enemy fire. To attempt it was to court death. One young engineer crawled out between the barbed wire, succeeded in repairing the severed wires, and was shot to pieces. Communication between men in the front line and the unseen leadership at headquarters was restored once again: but it had cost the life of this courageous man. Jesus, in a far more profound sense, restored

79

communications between men and God, communications that had been wantonly ruptured by human self-will. He achieved it at the cost of going to the cross. There's self-giving love for you.

The other example comes from *The Miracle on the River Kwai*, one of the most remarkable stories of the Second World War. The conditions for Allied prisoners in the Japanese prisoner-of-war camp on the River Kwai were so abysmal, and the mortality so high, that the men became almost bestial in their selfishness. They did not shrink from stealing food from their dying mates in a desperate attempt to survive. Ernest Gordon, who wrote the book, was himself given up as incurable by the M.O., but was nursed back to life by the devoted self-sacrifice of a man in his Company, Dusty Miller. But the 'miracle' was the transformation of attitudes in that camp as people in it began to understand and respond to the love of Christ. How did that begin to get through to men in such desperate conditions? It all started with a Scotsman, Angus McGilvray, who literally gave his life for his friend. The friend was very ill and about to die. Someone had stolen his blanket. Angus gave him his own. Someone had stolen his food. Angus gave him his own. The result? Angus's friend got better. But Angus collapsed one day from starvation and exhaustion. He just pitched on his face and died.

The story spread round the camp like wildfire. How was it that a man could give himself for another like that? They recalled the words of Jesus: 'Greater love has no man than this, that a man lay down his life for his friends.'[1] And they began to understand something of what the cross of Jesus meant. For he had not only given his life for his friends, as Angus, inspired by love for Jesus, had done for his friend. But Jesus had given his life that his *enemies* should live, and live with the very life of God inside them. And gradually throughout that camp men came to hand over their lives to Jesus. The results were tremendous and

[1] John 15 : 13.

lasting. They had seen in Angus genuine love, and love is unselfish, sacrificial. It is also challenging: which brings me to my last characteristic of genuine love.

5. Love is challenging
But in a very remarkable way. For love does not go round asking for response – not if it is real love. Love is accepting. That is why it is so liberating. It is a marvellous thing to know that you are accepted by someone else, warts and all. But when that happens, it is because the lover sees something attractive in the one he loves. It is, partly at any rate, because the loved one deserves the love of the lover. But not with God. He loves us, not because we are lovable, but because he is love. Not because we deserve it at all, but because he is grace. And grace means, quite precisely, free love. Utterly undeserved by us, and utterly freely bestowed by him, with no strings attached. He will go on loving us whether we turn to him or not. His is an accepting love. A love so humble that he is willing to accept the tiniest fag-end of our lives; as he did with the penitent thief who responded to the grace of Christ almost with his last breath.

> 'Between the saddle and the ground
> He mercy sought, and mercy found.'

The grace of God accepts the unacceptable. And that is free love indeed.

But, perhaps all the more so because it makes no overt demands, such love is intensely challenging. It waits for us, it pleads with us, and that is bound to have some effect on us. It will either win us, or harden us.

In the late 1940s a gunman called Ezio Barberi became notorious in Italy as a cold-blooded killer, and leader of a celebrated gang which raided banks and jewellers, shooting down any who came between them and their loot. He was arrested in 1949, sentenced to 57 years of imprisonment, and committed to the maximum security wing of the San Vittore prison in Milan.

Although he was universally execrated, this man was loved by one person, a girl of seventeen whom he had never met. Maria Soresina started to keep a scrapbook of Ezio's escapades and crimes. She carried the book around with her and went to church each day to pray for him. She began to write to him regularly in jail. She understood him when nobody else did. She really cared. She pleaded with him. She loved him although he was not in himself the least bit lovable.

Gradually Barberi changed. Being on the receiving end of love like that began to make a new man of him. He had already been involved in organizing one mutiny in the prison, but his attitude changed. His violent ways began to disappear. He exchanged the pin-ups on his wall for a picture of Maria. He replied to her letters with a tenderness that he had never shown to anyone or anything before. Was this the hate-filled gangster of Milan?

The new Barberi became a model prisoner. He took a leading part in arranging and carrying out social and charitable events, and working voluntarily in the prison hospital. Love had challenged him, melted him, won him. And on 18 June 1968, twenty-one years after Maria had fallen in love with him, they were married in the prison chapel. Wooed by a love that sought him although he deserved hate, Ezio had responded positively to the implied challenge such love carried. Had he turned his back on it, it would merely have hardened him further.

What will you do with God's free love? He loved you before you ever knew anything about him. He loves you in your rebellion against him, in your estrangement from him. But the very patience, the acceptance of that love carries a tremendous challenge. Will you respond to it, as Ezio did to Maria's? In that case, you will be warmed and changed by it. Or will you turn a deaf ear to love's welcome, to love's pleading, to love's sacrifice – and so become harder and more cynical? It is up to you. But be clear about this. Nobody drifts into a relationship of love with the heavenly lover. It requires a decisive act of will on your part, just as it did on his part to provide any gospel for you to respond to. He did not drift into the incarnation, into the atonement. You, too, must decide.

In the Church of England Marriage Service, the minister asks the bridegroom, 'Wilt thou have this woman to thy wedded wife? Wilt thou love her, comfort her, honour, and keep her in sickness and in health; and, forsaking all other, keep thee only unto her, so long as ye both shall live?' The man says, 'I will.'

In her turn the bride is asked, 'Wilt thou have this man to thy wedded husband? Wilt thou obey him, and serve him, love, honour, and keep him in sickness and in health; and, forsaking all other, keep thee only unto him, so long as ye both shall live?' Again, she replies, 'I will.' Then, and not until then, their vows recited, are their hands joined together and they are married.

It is very like that with the love relationship between the heavenly bridegroom and the sinner – and that is not my analogy; it is used by Paul, and Hosea, Jeremiah and various other Bible writers. It is a wonderful picture. It is as if Christ is asked, 'Will you have this sinner as your bride? Will you love her and comfort her, honour and keep her, in sickness and in health?' and he says, 'I will.'

The question now comes fairly and squarely to us. Will you, designed by the Almighty to be bride of the heavenly lover, 'Will you have Jesus to your husband? Will you obey him and serve him, love him and honour him, whatever the circumstances of the future may hold?' With your 'I will' the contract is complete. The married life, linked indissolubly with the Lord, can begin. Has it begun? Will it? The choice rests with you.

4 Free world

Towards a new society

Cause for protest

'Now that you've been here a month,' said a Maidenhead man to a Saudi-Arabian visitor to Britain, 'what do you think of our TV?' 'It is almost perfect,' replied the Arabian gentleman. 'The good men beat the bad men in almost every programme. All you must work on now is the news.'

That's precisely the problem. Our society is in a mess. That is the main reason for the protest movement. It seems to many young people today that the destinies of the world lie in the hands of middle-aged governments out of touch with reality. It seems that the world is set on a course heading to destruction. We are appalled by the inequalities between rich and poor; the rich get richer and the poor poorer. This applies to countries as well as individuals. We look at the strikes, the inflation, the inertia, the boredom; we see the social injustice, the gross inefficiencies of mutton-headed bureaucracy, the concrete jungles erected by the town planners and architects. Is it any wonder that there is protest?

And the older generation cannot understand it. They escape from the horror of modern life by means of gin and tranquillizers. And they find it incomprehensible that their young should turn to drugs! In an uncertain and unsafe world the parents seek security through possessions, and become increasingly acquisitive and materialistic. They cannot understand how their children, coming from such good homes, too, could possibly drop out from the rat race, the worship of mammon, and the steady job which had been thought the key to purposeful and satisfying living.

Is it surprising that the young realize the mess society is in, and are determined to change it? Is it surprising that even in sleepy old Britain the possibility of violent revolution can no longer be discounted? I was intrigued recently to see how one journalist had collected the promises of the last five American Presidents given in their Inaugural Addresses, promises about what they would achieve. In each case a new deal, new horizons, a new frontier, a new and more just society were what was offered. But the pace of progress, if it exists at all, has been depressingly slow. No wonder that the New Left refuse to wait for Godot. A new and more direct, more violent way of political action is everywhere apparent. Governments are blackmailed by hijackings and abductions; campuses are wrecked; politicians are roughed up; there have even been occasions of mild assault on the floor of the House of Commons! The Underground, with singers like Bob Dylan and Jim Morrison, urge revolutionary tactics:

'The old get older and the young get stronger
They got the guns, but we've got the numbers.
We're going to win, we're taking over
We want the world and we want it now.'

What is a Christian to say to all this social unrest of unprecedented proportions that is going on all round him? Is he to throw in his hand uncritically with the Left? Or is he to join the Conservative Party at prayer?

The Christian dilemma
Clearly the Christian cannot simply identify himself with the Establishment of the day. With the example and

85

teaching of Jesus behind him he cannot acquiesce in a situation where the rich get richer and the poor get poorer. He cannot accept the materialistic and selfish values of capitalism. He cannot say a pious 'Amen' to the conditions in Brazil where 10% of the population own 90% of the land, nor to the conditions in England where the poorer workers have to carry their strike for wages to the extent of crippling the nation before they are granted an increase which is derisory compared with what some of the monied classes win in a day on the Stock Exchange. You can't expect a man or woman imbued with the ideal of Christian freedom to agree with all that.

And yet, all is not well with the Left. The fallacies, the hypocrisies are not all to be found in one camp.

Is it not true that we are good at protest, but poor at suggesting alternative policies that are viable and positive? It is much easier to knock down than to build. Much modern protest hovers on the brink of aimless anarchy.

Is it not the case that we are good at talking about peace, but not very impressive at living in peace? The Left is not known for its harmony, any more than the Right is celebrated for its social conscience. Is there not a curious irony in the violent demonstrations for peace to which we have been subjected in recent years in many countries of the world? Will violence in London stop violence in Vietnam?

Is it not fair to say that we are good at hammering social injustice in South Africa and the United States, but remarkably adept at condoning it in China, Russia or Guinea? Was there as much protest about the Russian invasion of Czechoslovakia in 1968 as there was about the proposed South African cricket tour of England in 1971? If not, why not? The answer must be that we are highly selective, not to say hypocritical, in our protest.

There is much to attract the Christian idealist in the Left's concern for an equitable State. But there is much to repel. The ruthless liquidation of people who stand in the way of 'progress'; the reign of terror conducted by Trotsky,

86

by Lenin, by Stalin in pursuit of doctrinaire ends; all this is the very antithesis of Christian love, Christian freedom.

Some may recall what Peter Fryer wrote, when he was sent out by the *Daily Worker* to inspect the situation in Hungary first-hand, and report on the Rising in 1956. 'Socialist Hungary's new born freedom – one week old – was tragically destroyed. Freedom fighters were rounded up by the hated Secret Police, the notorious AVO. Communists, Socialists, Liberals alike were shot in their hundreds. Premier Nagy and his companions were given a worthless safe-conduct, tricked into custody, then "tried", sentenced and executed before the world Labour movement had been given the chance to protest or appeal for clemency.' Fryer, himself at that time a Communist, was disgusted by the Russians' utter cynicism, tissues of lies, and reign of terror.

Indeed, there is a curious parallel between Fascism and extremist Socialism of this type. Both are thoroughly ruthless in the pursuit of their ideal, irrespective of justice or personal compassion. Both can look impressive from outside. Benito Mussolini said, 'Democracy has taken away the sense of style from the life of the people. Fascism brings back a sense of style to the life of the people, that is a line of conduct, colour, the picturesque, the unexpected, the mystic.' It is illuminating to read a comment on the French student riots in Paris in 1968 by a British journalist of the Left: 'Above all, the French movement has style, a certain elegant flourish to all that it does, which catches the heart and makes one appreciate that politics is not just utilitarian science, but also an art.' That is how close Fascism can be to Communism. Remember Orwell's *1984*.

When you come down to it, there is an astonishing *naïveté* about human nature to be found in many of the pictures painted for us by the Left about the new society we are being urged to strive for. Rebellion against the old ways and the old ideals and the old leaders I can understand. What beats me is the amazing arrogance and self-deception of some of today's Protest men. They really seem

87

to think that they can concoct the ideal society, or at least make a very much better showing at it than their predecessors. Such arrogance is not new. It is as old as Homer's 'We are much better than our fathers'. And it is equally misplaced. It fails to take seriously the wickedness of human nature. And policies that fail to reckon with that are heading for disappointment. This is the surd in all Utopian schemes. Any future organization of society is bound to be made up of sinful men and women. It is bound to carry within it the seeds of it own destruction.

The basic fallacy in Socialism is to think you can change society without changing human nature, to think you can have a renewed community without renewed people. Few have the honesty and perception to echo G. K. Chesterton's famous letter to *The Times* when a correspondence was raging over what was wrong with the world. He wrote simply, 'Sir, I am. Yours faithfully, G. K. Chesterton.' But it was for people that had this courage, perception and honesty, that Jesus Christ came. 'I came not to call the righteous, but sinners' was his manifesto.[1] 'From inside, out of a man's heart, come evil thoughts . . . envy, slander, arrogance, folly'[2] was his analysis. He came to bring radical action to bear, to attack the problem of unjust society at its root in the human heart.

That is why the Christian revolution never starts with society as such, but with the individual.

The Jesus revolution
Jesus' programme was outlined in a song Mary his mother sang after his birth.[3] It is as radical as the Red Flag, and far more profound. 'Tell out, my soul, the greatness of the Lord, rejoice, rejoice, my spirit, in God my Saviour.' Why? Because he is going to change things. There will be a *social* revolution. 'He has brought down monarchs from their

[1] Mark 2 : 17.
[2] Mark 7 : 21.
[3] Luke 1 : 46–53.

thrones, but the humble have been lifted high.' There will be an *economic* revolution. 'The hungry he has satisfied with good things; the rich he has sent empty away.' This is all to be based upon a *spiritual* revolution, deep down in the hearts of members of the new society. 'The one who has put to rout the arrogant of heart and mind, shows sure and tender mercy to those in each generation who trust him. Holy is his name. Yet he is willing to be called *my* Saviour.'

That revolutionary programme Jesus began to carry out in his short ministry. After his death and resurrection it snowballed. Having crucified him as a Messianic pretender, both the Jewish and Roman authorities heartily hoped that they had seen the last of Jesus and his movement. But it didn't work out like that. A handful of men and women who had followed him, their hopes dashed, their convictions in ruins, were within a few weeks quite transformed. They maintained with inflexible assurance that Jesus was alive again; the grave had not sufficed to hold him down. They did so loudly and joyfully in the streets, which was inconvenient. They did so publicly in front of the chief priests, which was embarrassing, because those worthies could not deny it. The body was nowhere to be found. And to be sure, neither the Jewish nor the Roman authorities had moved it. That was the last thing they would dream of doing. Having got him where they wanted at last they would not be so asinine as to lend colour to any claims about a resurrection. Presumably, therefore, the disciples had taken the body away. Unfortunately, they did not act that way. These men, who had deserted Jesus in his hour of need, now found themselves possessed of a new courage. They were prepared to defy the religious authorities, who had the power to execute them – whereas previously they had blanched and slunk away at a serving girl's suggestion that they even knew Jesus of Nazareth. Something had clearly happened. Five hundred people claimed that they had seen Jesus risen. All the disciples were sure of it, even Thomas who was so hard to convince, and James the very brother of Jesus, who had thought him mad during his ministry. The most notable convert of all to this new movement was Saul of Tarsus, its leading opponent.

It was undeniable that something tremendous had happened to these men. Put them in prison for their beliefs and they merely sang psalms at midnight, and baptized their gaolers. Let them out, in sheer desperation, and they continued preaching the same message of a risen Jesus for which they had been imprisoned. They were so full of joy and confidence that there was some talk of their being drunk. But this explanation would not do. There was no hangover, and the changed lives persisted. Cowards became brave, immoral men chaste. Gloomy men gained joy. Impatient men became suffused with love. The more you tried to repress this movement the more it grew. They claimed that the difference in their relationships and behaviour could be very easily explained. The Jesus who had died, had risen again. One of the purposes of this fantastic thing was so that he could come and indwell the very lives of his believers. God would no longer be sought in temples, but in the changed lives of those who had offered him the temple of their body. They were nicknamed 'Christians', because they attributed the change to Christ; they talked about Christ; they were devoted to Christ; he was the centre of their lives and of their movement. Nothing else sufficed to explain the transformation – except the living indwelling presence of Christ himself. 'I live,' said Paul, 'yet it is no longer I. Christ lives inside me, and the life that I now lead I live by trusting the Son of God who loved me and gave himself for me.'[4] That went for them all.

The new society

The fact is that Christ's purpose in all this was not merely to change the lives of individuals, but to build up a new society. And that is precisely what happened. In the pages of the Acts of the Apostles, we find the Christian movement

[4] Galatians 2 : 20.

embracing an ex-medium, an erstwhile gaoler, a Roman proconsul, merchants with a big, world-wide business, a leading Rabbi, the most respected Jewish leader in Jerusalem, rich and poor, slave and free, male and female, all bound into a new community because they had been accepted by God for Christ's sake. All were recipients of a love they had done nothing to deserve and could never repay, the love of God that led Jesus to the cross of Calvary. This bound them together in a partnership which nothing could destroy. They saw the Christian society as a new temple, so to speak, built on the foundation of Jesus Christ, and every member a stone in that temple, related alike to the foundation and to all the other stones. The result was a society in which God was seen to dwell. Or they described it as a body in which every limb had its different function, but the whole organism harmoniously served the purposes of the risen and ascended Head. Though now invisible, he expressed himself through his Body, the new society, the community of the resurrection. Such was his plan, his plan for society, to work from the inside outwards; to change the lives and motivation of the redeemed individuals in order to build up a redeemed community. And that remains the Christian concept of a free society – men and women freed from self-centredness by Christ and related to one another in him.

Needless to say, Christians have not always lived up to that. We remain fallible human beings. Heirs of heaven, we are still citizens of earth. Equipped as we are with the Holy Spirit, we are not overpowered by him: our free choice enables us to give way to very different spirits. Christians retain the autonomy of their lives. If they choose to return to slavery to evil habit, God will not stop them.

Despite their failures, however, the individuals who made room for the risen Jesus began to grow in moral stature and social concern. They began to break down the barriers of wealth, citizenship, education and sex which stratified ancient society. They seemed to regard the slave as a brother in Christ, to be willing to endanger their own life for the chance of helping people infected with plague, to live peacefully within the laws of the State even when that State persecuted them to death. The Christian community, in short, grew so notably and so impressively that within a few generations it had laid siege to the whole Roman Empire. And the politically jaded, the morally bankrupt and the socially hidebound came to find in Christ the key to the new society where God is at work from within, slowly and gradually pervading it all like yeast.

That society has continued through the centuries. Sometimes it has been almost unrecognizable through the blindness, stubbornness and selfishness of its members. Sometimes it has become almost equated with a decadent establishment, as in Czarist Russia. Sometimes it has been almost indistinguishable from Liberal Humanism (as in Britain in the thirties) or a right-wing Fascism (as in Germany in the same period). The fallibility of this Christian community is all too apparent. It is, after all, made up of sinners. But those sinners are, if their allegiance to Christ is real and not nominal, people who have been forgiven at infinite cost, people who are indwelt by the Holy Spirit, people with whom he pleads, people whom he rebukes and woos and teaches – people whom he is trying to change from one degree of Christlikeness to another. Such is God's plan for society. He wants to show what he can do with rough material when it is put into his hands. The master carpenter of Nazareth is still at work among his people, chipping away, cutting back, polishing, until something of his own likeness begins to be visible in us, society and individual alike. It takes time. It is never complete this side of the grave. It requires the glad co-operation of every one of us. But it is real. And it is revolutionary. And the Christian hope for society in the future of this global village of ours is intimately bound up with the impact of Christian groups all over the world showing in their lives and relationships the liberation Christ brings, and acting as ginger groups in the countries to which they belong towards a truly egalitarian, truly supranational society based not upon domination but on love.

There is an interesting article in the *International Review of Mission* for January 1971 which tells of the enquiries made by C. F. Andrews, a young missionary in Delhi, among a number of leading Indian converts. What had attracted them to the Christian faith? It was not the longing for personal salvation. In almost every case, it was concern about the community. Some had believed because of the Christian moral standard, as set out in the Sermon on the Mount, and as lived out by Jesus of Nazareth. This was the ideal for all men everywhere, and it could be achieved only through allowing Christ to come and take up residence within. Others said that it was the freedom of the Christian family which impressed them – the attraction of the fellowship in Christ as compared with the bondage of caste. No force but Christ's has been able to break caste in India; no force but Christ's succeeded in demolishing the social barriers in the ancient world either. A third group were drawn to the Christian faith by the thought of Christ uniting into one the divided races and peoples of India. That is to say, the comprehensiveness and the warmth of the new society spelt hope to them for the humanization of man, for the future of mankind on this planet. The gospel of the crucified and risen Jesus brought them into the fellowship of the church and enabled them to see the unity in Christ which they then experienced as the first instalment of what human society should and could be.

It is so difficult to recapture a sense of the power of the Christian community when you live in the West, a West influenced for centuries by Christian ideals, but a West where all sorts of paganisms have been brought into the life of the church, and where the Christian community has often been lost in the churchly Establishment. Perhaps it is easier to get the feel from somewhere like Indonesia, where there is at present a large-scale turning to Christianity from nominal Islam and animism. An Indonesian pastor explained it like this: 'The language Christians used in their encounter with other faiths is not a language of hate, envy or pride. Enquirers could see in the dedication of Christians to their religious duties both joy and freedom. They could also see that Christian clergymen were really looking after their people, even those in the most remote villages. The Christian communities were concerned to help those who were suffering, especially widows and orphans. They could also see peace and joy in Christian families where father, mother and children eat together, pray together and sing together. Wives were treated with dignity by their husbands. They could also see the way in which Christians live together in communities. These communities witnessed to self-discipline and solidarity.' No wonder that many of those who were converted, on being asked the reason for their decision, replied, 'I really don't know. There is a kind of secret power which has made me join the church.' They had seen a new society, and were attracted to its Architect, Jesus Christ himself.

The other day I saw a cinema poster advertising a film with a fascinating title. It was 'Start the Revolution without me'! Now the Christian motto for a truly free society is the prayer 'Start the Revolution *within* me', and provided that is done, the practical outworkings can to some extent look after themselves. You see, the Christian has no doctrinaire and monolithic blueprint for the ideal society. The cause of man – and therefore the cause of Christ – may be furthered now by the Left, now by the Right, and now by some unlikely looking political coalition. Agents of the new society will not form a Christian party; they will be in all political parties, which they will select according to their conscience. The Christian will always want to ask himself, 'Which of the political options open to me is the most calculated to bring about the love between men, the justice, the trust, the responsibility that as Christ's free man I want to see?' His particular political affiliation will be determined by the answer he gives to that question. He will respect Christians in other parties who believe that their programme is more calculated to bring about the desired result. He will realize that no political party can change men's hearts, and that therefore all it can do is to provide a structure within which justice, freedom, care and responsibility can flourish. Accordingly, he will not be one to say 'My party right or wrong'. For the Lord's free man is ultimately tied to no political party, having an overriding loyalty to the Liberator himself. It is he alone who makes possible the new society, the revolution of love. So, above all else, the Christian will seek to please and follow Jesus, in the political sphere as everywhere else.

Towards a new world

The contemporary crisis
But our troubles do not end with society. Our very habitat is threatened today as never before.

We are threatened by the rising crime rate all over the world. There seems to be a direct relation between the growth of city life and the rise of crime. All over the world there is a growth of city life. . . .

Despite the 'men like gods' school, men refuse to behave like gods. One in seven marriages ends in divorce in Britain today; one in six children is illegitimate. In 1870 there were rather less than 2,000 indictable crimes per million of the population of Britain. Now there are 18,000. And the future? Well, work it out for yourself. Thirty per cent of all convicted persons are under the age of 17!

We are threatened by the population explosion. Not daunted by the fact that two-thirds of its population is beneath the bread line, the world's population is increasing at a phenomenal rate. If current trends continue it will be twice the present level by the year 2000 AD. It is rising fastest in the most backward countries, and the inevitable corollary is that unless something is done about it, they will fall still further behind economically.

We are threatened with the consumption and exhaustion of our resources in this planet. Some have calculated that we are using up petroleum and mineral reserves at such a rate that, if the annual increase continues, they will run out about the year 2000 AD or a little later. We are heading towards a situation where the whole of our urban way of life may well end within the lifetime of some people alive today – 'in a succession of famines, epidemics, social crises and wars', to quote the team of distinguished ecologists in their *Blueprint for Survival*.

In the mean time, we are facing a further threat, the pollution of our environment. The rivers are fouled with untreated sewage and chemical effluents; more than 20,000 miles of surveyed rivers in England are officially declared polluted. The Tees, which once boasted salmon, now boasts 500 discharge outlets of untreated sewage, while thousands of tons of sewage go directly into the sea near coastal resorts. Marine life throughout the oceans of the world has been hit by the accumulations of DDT deposited in the sea, whilst on land it has left a wilderness in place of the butterflies, birds and flowers which used to be there – along with the pests DDT was invented to kill. The atmosphere is polluted with nuclear fall-out and industrial fumes. Six million tons of sulphur dioxide, particularly dangerous for bronchial conditions, are pumped into the air of Britain each year. In this plastic, disposable age, the country is in danger of suffocating under its own rubbish: we produce at present some 17 million tons of domestic rubbish a year, double that of twenty years ago, and each year the proportion of indestructible plastic leaps dangerously. We are heading for a dustbin jungle in the midst of an ever-expanding concrete megalopolis.

Then there is the nuclear threat. Ever since that fateful day in August 1945 when the Allies dropped an atomic bomb on Hiroshima, it has been impossible to put the clock back. Man has lived in the knowledge that he can destroy organized existence on this planet. And every year more and more nations are joining the Nuclear Club. When is some fool, pushed beyond breaking point by motives of greed, retaliation or frustration, going to push the button and unleash upon mankind a nuclear holocaust? It would be frighteningly easy to do. The world came within a hair's breadth of it during the Cuba crisis. Living with this nightmare is one of the causes for the attitude 'Let us eat and drink, for tomorrow we die' – which today is a far more deeply seated eudaemonism born of despair than ever it was to the old Epicureans whose tag Paul quotes.

More recently the poor man's atomic bomb has emerged – a type of germ weapon more destructive than anything ever conceived before. It has been calculated that five ounces of a tasteless, colourless substance, botulinus toxin, in the drinking water could obliterate the whole population of Britain or the United States!

Is there a future for man?

Is there a future for *homo sapiens*? Christians claim humbly yet confidently that there is. We believe with the optimists in contemporary society that man has the means to cope with this crisis, if he will. Man is indeed wonderful. Because of his origin with God and his destiny with God, he is infinitely precious. But we cannot go all the way with the optimists. We know that there is a tragic twist in human nature, a twist that could at any time erupt into final and irreversible chaos.

However we must take issue with the pessimists, too, in our society. While we share with them the disinclination to put too much confidence in man's ability to run his environment responsibly and unselfishly, and to handle with discretion the tremendous powers put into his hands by modern science, we shall not join the Doomwatch boys. It is not true that there is no future for man. It is not true that human nature is incapable of change. There is hope for a world trembling on the brink of dissolution.

Begin with the secret

There are two ways of reading an Agatha Christie thriller. You can begin at the beginning, and plough straight through: in that case you will probably fail to spot the criminal. Or you can turn to the last but one chapter and find out who committed the crime! Apprised of the secret, you can then go back through the book and read the story from the start, picking up the clues you would otherwise have missed. And you can go on to the end and see how it all turns out.

It is, I think, rather like that with the book of human history. The Christian way of reading it is to begin, not at the beginning, nor even at the end, but with the secret. And the secret is Jesus. The key to the story of man is what God has done in and through Jesus crucified, risen and exalted. You can then turn back to the beginning. In the beginning God created everything through this same Jesus. 'Without him was not anything made that was made.'[5] Once I grasp that, I begin to realize the value of the universe. It is not the product of blind chance, the only star among the nebulae which happened to have the conditions on it which made life possible. No, it is the creation of a personal God who made men in his likeness, and when they rebelled, came in person to win them back.

As the disciples reflected on the significance of the cross and resurrection and saw Jesus bearing the filth of human sin, enduring the worst that man could do to him, and still rising again victorious – then they grasped the clue to the whole mystery. Truth, ultimate truth, loves. Truth comes in person. Truth suffers. Truth goes to the gibbet. But truth does not stay on the gibbet. Truth came down from the cross, out from the tomb, alive, triumphant, unquenchable.

And on that cross and resurrection, firmly anchored in

[5] John 1 : 3.

98

history 1,900 years ago, is built the whole of Christian optimism about the future. The crucified and risen Jesus at the centre of history gives meaning to the start of the story, and gives assurance about the end. The future is controlled by one who holds the keys of death and the life beyond. The one who endured in his own person the full onslaught of the forces of evil, suffering and disintegration, has overcome. 'The Lamb once slain', to use the evocative language of the Apocalypse, 'sits in the midst of the throne of God.'[6] The key to his plan for the world, the pledge of the future awaiting man and his habitat, is to be found in that strange figure, crucified and risen. We have in the cross and the resurrection of Jesus a trailer, so to speak, of God's final picture. We have this solid, tangible clue to God's future for the world, a future to be worked out in history and transcending history.

The spring for action
That is what keeps the Christian hopeful about the future. But it does not make him complacent. He knows that God looks for our co-operation. So there can be no question of a Christian pietistically neglecting life on this earth in favour of 'pie in the sky when you die'. The Christian is committed to furthering humane conditions on this earth, while realizing that this life is not all there is. The very fact that I believe that the world and all mankind are created by God demands that I care both about my brother men and about the world God made.

The very fact that I believe man's destiny is a corporate one, which I cannot fully envisage, but which is described by the prophets in the Bible as 'a new heaven and a new earth in which righteousness dwells', demands that I get involved in seeking the welfare of my fellow men and our common habitat.

The very fact that my Bible teaches me that man is a product both of the 'dust of the earth' and of God breathing

[6] Revelation 5 : 12, 13.

his life into our biological frame[7] demands that I shall be as concerned about the one part of my nature as the other. My life with God matters. My life as a human being matters. The two are co-ordinate, and any Christianity which exalts the spiritual gospel above the social or vice versa is untrue to the teaching of Jesus.

And finally, I am driven to care about this world for the simple reason that I see man as God's viceregent in the ecological system. In the pictorial yet infinitely profound language of the book of Genesis, man is seen both as the climax of the created order, and as subject to the God who put him there. Man's destiny is to head up creation, but to do so not as autonomous but as one who will have to give account to the Creator. That is why as a Christian I cannot disclaim concern about what will happen to the world in the next generation. My responsibility to my Maker will not allow it.

For all these reasons the free man in Christ will wake up before it is too late, and will join with other men of vision and goodwill in bringing the seriousness of the ecological crisis to the constant notice of the leaders of the world. The means of dealing with our problems lie to hand. They are not beyond us. If we gave ourselves as a nation and as a globe to meeting the problems, they could readily be solved. But the trouble lies with man.

It would be perfectly possible for the factories to treat their effluents and make them harmless before discharging them into the rivers and the sea – but it would be expensive, and the profit margin would go down. It would be perfectly possible to have clean air – at a price. It would be possible to curb population growth if as a world we set our mind to it. It would be possible to meet the food shortage if self-sacrifice were the order of the day. But it would demand a shattering reversal of priorities. For instance, it has been calculated that a child born in the USA will consume during his life at least twenty times as much as one born in India,

[7] Genesis 2 : 7.

and contribute about fifty times as much pollution to the environment. These things could be changed, if we wanted to.

The USA must have spent between thirty and forty billion dollars in the past decade to win the race to the moon, and the current defence expenditure of the great powers beggars description. Why should that money not be channelled into the far more important project of improving life on earth and solving the problems that threaten the continued life of man on this planet?

The know-how is there; the resources are there; but the will is not. It is the task of the Christian man and the Christian society both to keep informed as to what is threatening the world, and to press for truly human priorities to be kept uppermost in national and international policies.

We come back again and again to the human will. It is here that the battle must be fought, and can be won if, and only if, Jesus Christ is given entrance to the situation. He is the cosmic Christ, the creator, sustainer and goal of the universe. He is also the ideal for human life and the dynamic for living. He deserves to be trusted.

5 Free offer Free choice

THE TEACHING OF JESUS was packed with surprises. That is one of the reasons why people flocked to hear him. You never knew what exciting thing was going to emerge next. Nobody complained that his sermons were too long, too dull or too incomprehensible. He once told this memorable story in order to illustrate the freedom he had come to give.

'A man prepared a great feast and sent out many invitations. When all was ready, he sent his servant around to say to those who had been invited, "Come, for all is now ready." But they all began making excuses. One said he had just bought a field and wanted to inspect it. He asked to be excused. Another said he had just bought five pair of oxen and wanted to try them out. He asked to be excused. Another said, "I have just got married, and therefore I cannot come."

'The servant returned and reported to his master what they had said. His master was angry, and told him to go out quickly into the streets and the alleys of the city and to invite the beggars, crippled, lame, and blind. But even then, there was still room.

' "Well, then," said his master, "go out into the country lanes and out behind the hedges and urge anyone you find to come, so that the house will be full. For none of those I invited first shall taste my banquet." '[1]

[1] Luke 14 : 16–24.

An astounding invitation

If ever a story challenged the preconceptions of the hearers, this was it. I see here first of all an astounding invitation. 'Come,' says the host, 'Come.' God is like that. If there is one word which sums up the attitude of God towards mankind, it is this: 'Come.' I find it perfectly astonishing that the God I have disobeyed and neglected and snubbed and wronged should issue me with an invitation like this. In the word 'Come' I see to the real nature of God. He is not, after all, a cold judge saying 'Go' but a great lover saying 'Come'. All the way through the Bible God has shown himself in this light. It shines through the pages from Genesis to Revelation. 'Come into the ark,'[2] says God to Noah, for he does not want anyone to perish. 'Come,' says God, in the poetic imagery of Isaiah: why should you stay away from me and starve?

'Ho, every one who thirsts,
   come to the waters;
and he who has no money,
   come, buy and eat!
Come, buy wine and milk
   without money and without price.
Why do you spend your money for that which is not bread,
   and your labour for that which does not satisfy? . . .
Incline your ear, and come to me;
   hear, that your soul may live.'[3]

Jesus took up the same theme in his ministry. 'Come to me, all you who labour and are heavy laden, and I will give you rest.'[4] He did not want people to remain laden with the past and struggling with the present. The cure lay in coming to him.

In the book of Revelation this cry is reiterated many

[2] Genesis 7 : 1.
[3] Isaiah 55 : 1ff.
[4] Matthew 11 : 28.

times. The puzzled writer hears a voice from heaven, 'Come up here, and I will show you what is to come.'[5] The answer to his confusion about the destiny of mankind lies in coming closer to the heavenly Lord. And in almost the concluding words of the whole Bible, the Spirit of God unites with the church on earth to echo this princely invitation, 'Come. And let him who is thirsty come, let him who desires take the water of life without price.'[6]

Isn't this amazing? God, it seems, is not determined to keep himself to himself and conceal himself from us. He invites us into his presence: 'Come.' We are accustomed to supposing that we men hold the centre of the stage of life. By our researches we have banished God into the wings. All the same, we like to suppose that we are still honest seekers after God. We want to have our cake as well as eat it – or rather, eat it without having it! The theological whizz-kids write books like the one which came to my desk today with the striking sub-title, *Christian Faith Without Belief in God*. We may not express it in precisely this way, but the attitude such a book discloses is very widely held. Man holds the middle of the stage. God, if he exists, is a God who hides himself off-stage in the wings. We say that we'd love to find him if only we could. But it is all too difficult. Perhaps comparative religion will help us. Let's campaign to get it taught in schools instead of Christianity. Let's have a bit of Buddhist light here, and a spot of Hindu illumination there and Islamic reverence and Christian love and . . . Then perhaps we'll be able to get through to God, the God who hides himself.

But the truth disclosed in this remarkable story Jesus told is precisely the reverse of this. No doubt there is some light in other faiths. It would be strange indeed if there were not. But the shattering condemnation of man is that he does not follow such light as he has when he gets it. He

[5] Revelation 4 : 1.
[6] Revelation 22 : 17.

prefers to go on in the dark.[7] Our basic trouble is not that we do not know the light, but that we do not respond to what light we have. Jesus put it thus: 'this is the judgment (under which men lie), that the light has come into the world, and men loved darkness rather than light, because their deeds were evil.'[8] Evil? Surely that's a bit hard for respectable folk like us? No, simply honest.

The evil lies not so much in what we have said or done; though if our actions of the last twenty-four hours, to go no further, were flashed on a screen for all to see, I guess we'd feel a bit shifty. But the real evil lies in what we are – so twisted in our self-centredness that we do not come to the light when we see it, but prefer to go on in the dark. To return to our analogy: the case is not, as we fondly believe, that we are standing in the middle of the stage as honest seekers after a God who hides himself. God is in the middle of the stage, issuing the invitation to us to share life with him, to make room for him in our personalities, to come to his great banquet -- however you like to express it. He takes this invitation business so seriously that he did not merely send holy men and prophets to pass it on. He came himself to issue it. 'No, thank you,' said mankind – and shot off into the wings. Let's get it quite clear: we are the ones that are hiding ourselves. Not God.

It is a time-honoured procedure. When Adam in the Garden joined Eve in taking the forbidden fruit from the delightful tree of knowledge, when they got emancipated from degrading obedience to the Creator, they started hiding. That didn't stop the great Lover coming to look for them. 'And they heard the sound of the Lord God walking in the garden in the cool of the day, and the man and his wife hid themselves from the presence of the Lord God among the trees of the garden. But the Lord God called to the man, and said to him, "Where are you?" '[9] It wasn't

7 John 3 : 20.
8 John 3 : 19.
9 Genesis 3 : 8, 9.

man in the middle of the stage bewailing (or exulting in) an absentee God that was the trouble. It was a generous God walking the stage looking for runaway man. And so it has continued. It was like that in Jesus' day. There was nothing about his life to provoke opposition except its too radiant light. It showed up the darkness all around. And so the men of darkness either ran away from that light or tried to quench it. 'That was the true light, the light which gives light to every man, which was coming into the world.'[1] The great invitation was being issued to reluctant guests by one who ought by rights not to be issuing an invitation at all, but rather a sentence on his recalcitrant subjects.

A remarkable description

The next paradoxical point which strikes me about this story is the remarkable description it gives. The context in Luke's account makes it very plain that Jesus is trying to explain the nature of God's kingdom by this parable. How shall he describe it? Behaviour? Effort? Belief? No, none of them is adequate. A banquet! That is the word. And that was a great surprise to Jesus' first hearers. Shame upon us Christians, but it still does cause surprise both within the church and outside it. Ask people – those you may happen to meet in the street or the pub, for example – what they think Christianity is all about. And I bet you will look for a long time before you get any reply faintly reminiscent of a feast. Christianity is, people feel, solemn and kill-joy; earnest, rather narrow, dull, respectable. It is more than faintly hypocritical; it is not for the likes of us (anyhow, we're just as good as those who go to church!). It is a matter of long faces, black-bound prayer books, best clothes on Sunday . . .

I believe this is one of the most effective pieces of Satanic propaganda that the unthinking have swallowed in the so-

[1] John 1 : 9.

called Christian West. Christianity is dull, runs the propaganda. If you want an exciting life, steer clear of it.

Dull? *Dull?* Did anybody who knew him ever think that Jesus was dull? Did anyone ever think the apostles and the early Christians dull? Dull, as they got converted from crass paganism and immorality? Dull, as they proclaimed Jesus in the streets and market places even during times of persecution until the authorities came and took them away? Dull, as they shared out their belongings for the benefit of the needy? Dull, as they died for their beliefs, gored to death in the arena? These men claimed that they had found the pearl of great price in Jesus Christ. They had found treasure. They had discovered a new dimension to life, the life of the Age to Come – available here and now. They had personally accepted the invitation of God outlined long ago in Isaiah, the 'free wine and milk' of the feast which God provided. They had come to Jesus who gave them release from burdens and strength in their labouring. It was indeed a banquet for them, a party. And so the Christian life remains. It is joyful, satisfying.

Are you satisfied? I doubt it. Look at the faces going to work tomorrow in the bus or tube. Do they look satisfied? Look at the successful and the rich. Are they satisfied? Have the Onassis millions made Jackie Kennedy happy? Do you remember Talitha Getty? A woman of haunting beauty, talent and wealth. She had all the jewels, all the clothes that a woman could want. Belonging to the jet set, she married the son of the world's richest man, and after a honeymoon round the world settled in a palatial penthouse in Rome. Rich friends, wild parties and a leading role in *Barbarella* made up her life. It did not satisfy. She took an overdose of drugs and killed herself.

Always with people during life, she was alone in death. Her hearse was unaccompanied. Nobody was there to say a last farewell. There was not even a flower. The successful people, the beautiful people have time only for the living. Talitha was dead and forgotten.

Or take Lyle Stewart, uncrowned king of the world of American sex books. That man was such a success that of the first twenty-five books he published, twelve passed the million mark. That man gambles so big that 'they call me God in Las Vegas'. But money and success do not satisfy. He confessed, when his wife died, 'Money, success, it's all meaningless without her. I'm dead inside. I feel a thousand years old. I'm bored with so much, even with money.' That sentiment was echoed recently to me by a young man who is almost certainly a millionaire and whose name is known all over the world. 'I agree a hundred per cent that making money and winning success and fame give one zero satisfaction.'

Contrast that with this comment from a leading man in the insurance world who has recently discovered the feast of the Christian life. 'As I climbed into bed that night after inviting the Lord Jesus to take charge of my life, my heart was burning. This gave me confidence that I had done the right thing – although I was rather scared of where this decision would lead me. My wife found that it went over her head. She was sure that whatever it was that I had caught, it would not last. I also worried that I would not have the strength and perseverance to last as a Christian. I didn't know how to leave it with the Lord.

'Why did I ever doubt Jesus' promises that he would come and take charge? Reading John's Gospel for the first time in 27 years, using a modern translation, I was staggered by what it told me. I hungered to read more. I had so much to catch up. Encouraged by my new friends, I widened my reading. Me! – who previously had struggled to read one non-insurance book a year.

'I learned how to pray. It was difficult at first, but I found that the more I learned about Jesus Christ from the Bible, the easier it became to pray to him as a trustworthy friend and guide. It became a joy to pray not only at bedtime but when I met daily problems or temptations.

'Looking back over the past 16 months, the change I've

undergone is breathtaking. My sense of priorities is quite different. Yet, this period of time has been the most challenging and satisfying time in my business and personal life.

'I yearn to share this wonderful gift of life with others – especially with my family. My cup of joy will overflow when they, one by one, trust Jesus Christ as Lord and Saviour.' Since writing that, some of his family have come to share for themselves in the feast Christ provides.

Of course, this is no escape route from the problems of life. Your problems increase when you become a Christian, but you have someone to share them with. Listen to a man who, in his way, is discovering the satisfying nature of the Christian life although he suffers under the persistent malady of clinical depression. Some couple of years or so after his conversion from Buddhism to Christ, he wrote to me as follows:

'I have experienced God's love in a new, more refreshing, and far fuller manner than ever before. I think it is fair comment to say that I'm not the only one who has noticed it! I find that I can rejoice in everything. I've discovered a secret of success, which in some ways rather amuses me. At one time depressions were the plague of my life. Later, I came to accept them as part of my temperament and to "sit them out". *Now*, and here comes the amazing conclusion, I actually *praise the Lord for them*! For if my faith is to be strong only when I'm happy, then it's fairly insecure. A depression, on the other hand, puts it to the test, discovers what it's really worth, and in the end, I think, strengthens it. At the same time, I find, as I turn my eyes away from myself and towards the Lord, and praise him, the problem begins to dwindle immediately.'

It may be a remarkable description of the Christian life to see it as a feast, but it is true. The warmth of the atmosphere in the Christian banquet, the love of the Host, the companionship of the guests, the adequate provisions, all combine to satisfy our deepest needs for integration, pardon, purpose and peace of mind.

A surprising statement

There is a third shock for us in this story of the Great Supper. It is the surprising little statement, 'Come, for *all is now ready*.' The Jew of that day had a good deal in common with us. He believed that God would look after his country, and would look after him as well, provided he did his bit. And his bit meant being decent and kind, regular at worship, diligent in his standards of behaviour, strict in his keeping of the Law. Granted all this, he would be able to face his Maker without too great embarrassment on the last great day. The Almighty would weigh his good deeds against his failures, and, being a God of mercy, he would no doubt tip the scales enough to let him scrape through.

And here came Jesus proclaiming in scarcely veiled language that the good things of God's day of salvation were available now. 'Come, for all is *now* ready.' That was certainly a shock. It was difficult to take it in.

By those apparently innocent words, 'Come, for all is now ready,' Jesus was launching a frontal assault on this whole conception, as dear to the heart of a Jew as it is to us, that God ought to accept us because of our good deeds. What Jesus was emphasizing by this parable was that, however good you are, you are not good enough for God. Human rectitude is at best grey in the light of his dazzling character. Our very best actions are mixed in their motives. And very often, the better a man is, the more self-satisfied he is, and the less he senses his need of forgiveness. He wants to come before his Maker not on his knees, but on his two feet, confident not only of a welcome but that somehow God will be indebted to him for his decency in turning up. The Pharisees felt like that. They were good men, and my word, they knew it. It was in all probability such men that Jesus had in mind when he described the original men who had been invited to the party as making excuses for their unwillingness to come. Basically, they felt no hunger for the great supper. They were all right as they were, thank you very much.

Just imagine for a moment what heaven would be like if it were peopled by self-satisfied people like that. People who disdained others, people who felt God owed them something, people who were really interested only in themselves and their achievements. That wouldn't be heaven. It would be hell. That attitude can receive nothing from God. That is why 'none of those who were invited shall taste of my supper'. You can't enjoy the good things God offers until you acknowledge your need of them.

The amazing good news which Jesus brought and Jesus made possible means that God invites all and sundry into his great supper. The prime qualification for attendance is the recognition that we cannot earn our invitation, and cannot contribute to the good fare provided. God has prepared the feast for us. He would be insulted if we brought the crusts we had been hoarding as our entrance fee, so to speak, for the banquet. No. He has done all that is necessary to make possible our pardon and our peace; the strength to live well and the joy to bring happiness to others are all his gift. We can never earn such a banquet. We cannot contribute to it. We can simply accept it, or decline the invitation.

When Jesus died on the cross he cried 'Finished'. The task of putting us back in the right with God was complete. It needed no adding to. When Jesus rose again it was, among other reasons, so that he could live out his powerful, shining life, through his followers. So much so that Paul could say, 'I have been crucified with Christ: nevertheless I live; yet it is no longer I, but Christ living in me.'[2] Even in times of pain and distress he found Christ's companionship his strength. 'He said to me,' said Paul, describing God's reaction to his repeated prayer for the healing of an infirmity which he calls his 'thorn in the flesh', 'he said to me, "My grace is sufficient for you, for my strength finds its

[2] Galatians 2 : 20.

most complete expression in weakness." Most gladly will I therefore welcome my infirmities in order that the power of Christ may rest upon me.'[3]

In the kaleidoscope of experience that goes to make up life, Christians recognize that God is the host who provides the good things of the banquet. We can neither earn them nor contribute to them. They are not reserved for some vague future day. They are offered to us now. We receive them now or not at all. The theologians call this 'realized eschatology'. What was thought by the Jews of old to belong to the Last Day has been brought within our day and within our grasp by Jesus. He says to us: 'Look. In me you can find a friend who will never leave you, a master who can control you, a guide who can lead you through life. In me you can find the point of integration for your whole personality, including the forgiveness of the past, and the strength to be different in the future. Come, for all things are now ready.' You can never deserve all this. You can never find it anywhere else.

A staggering response

But there is a further surprise in store for us. And that is the reaction of the guests to the great invitation. They all began to make excuses. It looked fair enough – one had to go and see his farm and another his new oxen. And as for the man who had just got married, of course he couldn't go!

But when you look a little deeper the reasons show up for what they really are, excuses. Whoever would be such a fool as to buy a property without giving it a very thorough survey first? Who would be such an ass as to buy a new Lotus car without first giving it a road test? As for the man who had married his new wife, why not bring her to the party as well? Excuses, that's what they were. The real reason for their non-acceptance was quite different. They

[3]2 Corinthians 12: 9.

did not want to come. And they were making circumstances the excuse to cover basic unwillingness.

That's exactly what people do today: perhaps even you?

'I have no time', you say, 'to get interested in religion.' Just twenty-four hours a day, no more no less. Exactly the same as everybody else. You have time to do what you want in life. When you say 'I haven't got time', what you mean is 'My will is unyielded'. Then why not say so? It is much easier to sort out a problem if you have the honesty to admit what it is.

'I'm all right as I am. I never did anyone much harm.' All right as you are? If you were, do you think the Lord from heaven would have bothered to come to this earth and go to Calvary in order to bring you back to him? A man once approached Jesus and said, in effect, 'I'm all right as I am.' So, trying to be clever, he asked, 'Teacher, which is the great commandment in the law?' Jesus replied, 'You shall love the Lord your God with all your heart, and with all your soul, and with all your mind. This is the great and first commandment. And a second is like it: You shall love your neighbour as yourself.'[4] Have you kept that second commandment? Of course not. Have you kept the first commandment? Still less. Then what's all this about being all right as you are? You have broken the first and second commandments of God, the summary of your duty to him and to others. You are as much a failure as the criminal or flagrant sinner you despise.

'I'm not so sure that God exists,' says another. That, too, is an excuse. You call on him when you are in a fix, don't you? I'll tell you why you are not sure of God. Because you are out of touch with him. It's difficult to be sure of anyone when you can't see them and have no dealings with them. People came to Isaiah centuries ago with this problem. 'God seems so far away,' they complained. Listen to his reply. 'The Lord's hand is not shortened so that it cannot save. His ear has not become dulled so that it cannot hear.

[4] Matthew 22 : 36–39.

But your sins have separated between you and your God. And your wrongdoings have hid his face from you so that he will not hear.'[5] There's a barrier in the way. You are out of touch. That is why he seems to be so distant. Suppose you were sitting in the sunshine one day when thick nimbus clouds rolled up and covered the sky. Would you complain, 'I don't believe the sun exists any more. I can't see it. I can't feel it. It doesn't exist'? No, you would realize that something had come between. That is why you were no longer able to enjoy the light of the sun or bask in its warmth. And that is precisely what our sins have done to God: they have erected a barrier between us. No wonder he seems distant.

There is, however, a break in the cloud. The sun shines through that break upon a hill called Calvary and an empty tomb. And the invitation comes again, 'Come, for all is now ready.'

'But I'm not the religious sort,' you say; 'I have no faith.' Neither am I the religious sort, for that matter! Were the fishermen and tax men and harlots who made up the first Christian community? God is not just interested in the religious sort. Heaven forbid – he is not narrow minded! In point of fact it was the religious sort who on the whole declined to follow him. It was the religious sort who helped to crucify him. Don't let it worry you if you are not the religious sort. You will be all the more ready to let your Lord, once you come to know him, change the ordinary everyday sides of your life, and less likely to shut him away in a box labelled 'Religious. Highly dangerous except on Sundays'. It is quite untrue that you have no faith. Faith is not a feeling that is produced in certain types of believer. Faith is confidence produced by the reliability of the object. You exercise faith every time you sit down in a chair, every time you go to a doctor, entrust your affairs to a lawyer or go for a trip in a bus. You can't *know* beforehand that the chair won't break, the doctor won't poison you, the lawyer

[5] Isaiah 59 : 1, 2.

won't cheat you or the bus won't go in some non-scheduled direction. But you have reasonable grounds for confidence in all these cases. You take the risk of committing yourself in the light of the evidence. And you are not disappointed. Your assurance comes when, and only when, you do commit yourself. It's like that with Christ. There are reasonable grounds for profound confidence that he will accept you, transform your life, and never leave you. But you can't have the assurance of faith until you exercise it by trusting him and asking him to come and take you over, lock, stock and barrel. Faith, you see, has to do not only with understanding but experience.

'Ah, but I've tried it all before, and it makes no difference,' you say. Tried what before? It is all too easy to confuse personal faith in Christ with something superficially like it which may not necessarily involve the will in the same way. I have often found people who confuse it with confirmation. Now confirmation is the liturgical way in which churches which practise infant baptism provide for their young members to make the personal act of faith proper to full church membership. It is meant to be the opportunity for the person being confirmed to say, 'I am personally ratifying the promises made on my behalf at my baptism as a child. I do forsake sin. I do accept Christ. I do determine to follow him.' That is what it is meant to be; and for those who enter into this and mean it, the hands of the bishop laid upon their head with prayer for perseverance is a great encouragement and symbol of the fatherly hand of God upon them. But it is perfectly possible to be baptized and confirmed without any surrender of the will to God at all. I know. Because it happened to me.

Sometimes people confuse Christian faith with some time in life when they were in great danger or need, and called upon God, and in an unmistakable way he answered. Fine. But that does not mean you are a Christian from that day on. It is one thing to believe that God exists, and quite another to come to him as your Saviour and Lord and ask him to take control of the life he gave you, the life he died to redeem.

Sometimes, I find, people have gone to the front at a big evangelistic meeting and, maybe with tears in their eyes, have made some sort of response. But even this can be a counterfeit of the real thing. It is one thing to be moved even to tears. It is quite another to make your whole life over, as far as you know how, to Christ. The latter has a finality about it; the finality of committing yourself to someone else for life in marriage, or leaving your homeland and becoming a citizen of another. It's a death as well as a new life, an end as well as a beginning. It is, by definition, unrepeatable.

The important questions over this matter of Christian faith and commitment are not 'Do you feel different?' or 'Do you remember a time when you committed your life to our Lord?', but 'Have you got Christ? Has he got you? Do you know him? Are you enjoying his company now?' That is what matters – a personal relationship with Christ, beginning now and not ending this side of the grave; beginning in lonely isolation as you accept the invitation to the great supper, but issuing into the companionship of men and women of every conceivable race and background who sit as fellow guests at the banquet with you. Are you in or out of that banquet? These are the only two places you can be. And only you (and God) know which is true in your case.

An arresting sense of urgency

There is a further surprise waiting for us, as unexpected as when it assailed the ears of Jesus' first hearers. It is the sense of urgency about the invitation. Don't hang around in the streets, or skulk behind the hedges, it seems to say. Come, for all is now ready. *You* come. Come at once. Don't put it off. It won't be easier later on.

'But', you may say, 'I am a churchman.' So were those to

whom Jesus spoke that day. Better churchmen than you. Religious Jews prayed seven times a day. They gave God 10% of all their money, and many of them took this obligation so seriously that they extended it to the mint bushes in their back garden. If it comes to churchgoing we aren't in the same league as those folk. But those churchmen made excuses and stayed away. Those churchmen had hearts that rebelled against the free love of God who opened his home and his banquet to outsiders, though they were religious enough in all conscience. It is not difficult to worship God with your lips while your heart is far from him. But you will never discover any liberation that way. Formalism does not spell freedom. It is not difficult to understand the Christian message, recognize its appeal and validity and say to oneself, 'Yes, I must do something about it one day.' Remember, none who put off the invitation with their excuses, *none* of them, tasted the supper. Prevarication does not spell freedom.

But Jesus spells freedom. Free offer on his part. What remains but a free choice on ours? Be a man, then, and decide. Come off the fence. If there is no God, no personal origin to life, no future; if we are straws carried along on the flood of inexorable historical processes or are the playthings of sheer chance, then freedom is an illusion anyhow. But if the Christian account of the world is true, then your human personality is of infinite value. It is not the case that you are at the mercy of forces that cannot be withstood. They can. You are free to choose to accept your life as the gift of a loving Creator God who, incredible though it seems, offers you a free invitation to his banquet. You are free to reject his offer. He has done all he can, for he has offered you himself without reservation. Beyond that he cannot go without inhibiting the freedom he gave you. The response he looks for is that you should offer yourself back to him without reservation. Christ for me: I for Christ. That is the secret of Christian freedom.

A demanding cost

'Hold on,' I think I hear you saying. 'What about the stuff in small print? What is it going to involve?'

Sorry. I should have made that plain, at least as plain as is possible, before you take the plunge. Because, as with any relationship, it is impossible to say what it will cost you until you embark upon it. But at least a thumbnail sketch is called for. And, characteristically, Jesus gave one in the words that follow this matchless story of the Great Supper. Not surprisingly, we read that great crowds followed him. He turned round and gave them the solemn warning that following him was a costly business.

Jesus before family

'Anyone who wants to be my follower,' he said, 'must love me far more than he does his own father, mother, wife, children, brothers or sisters – yes, more than his own life – otherwise he cannot be my disciple.'[6] Tough words. Take them to heart. They mean in simple prose that Jesus is to come first. Loyalty to him may not readily be understood by other members of the family. Your parents may worry that you have got religious mania. Your wife may say, 'Poor thing – it'll wear off, I hope.' Your new way of life may well include opening up your home, and this may seem strange to others in the family. It may mean that you want to spend time in prayer, and this also will seem odd to them. It could mean a reassessment of your finances: and all these things can affect the family. My own job involves training men for the Christian ministry. A large number of our students over the years have told me of the opposition they have faced at home to being a whole-hearted Christian. It is all very well to go to church now and again (too frequently is unhealthy!). But to start bringing your Christianity into the home, and letting it determine your choice of career and life partner and so on – why, that is

6 Luke 14 : 26.

going much too far. You're wasting your education and talents, my boy! Yes, it is still tough to follow Jesus, tough at home. Are you prepared for that?

Jesus before self

It's tough in another way, too. 'No one can be my disciple,' said Jesus, 'who does not carry his own cross and follow me.'[7] That's an odd thing to say, isn't it? Today the cross is something girls wear round their necks on a nice little chain. Or it is some ailment, arthritis maybe, of which Granny says, 'It's my cross, I suppose.' That is assuredly *not* what Jesus meant. The cross was a common sight in Palestine under the Roman occupying forces. It was something for dying on. It was a cruel death, a shamefully exposed death, a lingering death. His hearers must have been shocked when Jesus said, 'No one can be my disciple who does not carry his own cross and follow me.' He meant them to be shocked, for he wanted to get them to count the cost of discipleship. It is no bed of roses. If you want an easy life, steer clear of that strange man on his cross.

To follow him will mean that, like Jesus, you will have to die. Die to that selfishness, that self-will, those rights of yours, that comfortable time you like. All through your life Jesus will be summoning you to die with him. It will be a lingering death – because the 'I' in us is so arrogant, so utterly self-centred. It will be a public, exposed death, too, in a way. We are called to an open discipleship (and you can't conceal the state of affairs when you are carrying a whacking great cross on your shoulders). We are called on to have the courage of our convictions and not be ashamed of our Christianity. Christians have a trade name for it, repentance. It means letting the old rebellious self in all its manifestations be nailed to the cross, so to speak; in order that the resurrection life of the risen Lord shall take us over. No repentance...no Christian life. No dying with Christ... no sharing his life. It's as basic as that. And as costly. I'm

[7] Luke 14 : 27.

still trying to learn in practice what it means. And he is still showing me great areas of my life that are not yet yielded to his control.

Three questions to face
As if that imagery were not vivid enough to set us thinking, Jesus goes on to ask, in effect, three questions.

Can you keep it up? The Christian life is just what it says, a Christian *life*. It is a long-distance race, not a sprint. Are you prepared for that? Will you make him Lord of the years that lie ahead? If not, you're asking for trouble. 'Don't begin until you count the cost. For who would begin construction without first getting estimates and then seeing if he has enough to pay the bills? Otherwise he might complete only the foundation before running out of funds. And then how everyone would laugh.'[8]

Can you face a fight? That's Jesus' second question. 'What king would ever dream of going to war without first sitting down with his counsellors, and discussing whether his army of 10,000 is strong enough to defeat the 20,000 men who are marching against him?'[9] The Christian life is a battle. A lifelong fight against evil in myself, society, and the devil himself. If I take on Jesus Christ as my Lord, I take on the devil as my enemy. And it becomes a battle. To be sure, Christ promises to put at my disposal the boundless resources of his risen life, so that, like Paul, I may be able to cry, 'I can do anything through him who gives me power.'[1] But what's the use of that if I am not prepared to join the fight?

Can you endure to be in a minority? Because you will be, if you follow Christ. That has never deterred men and women

[8] Luke 14 : 28f.
[9] Luke 14 : 31.
[1] Philippians 4 : 13.

worth their mettle, but it is a fact of life that needs to be carefully considered all the same. You will always be up against the odds. You will always be in the position of that king with 10,000 facing opposing forces of 20,000. Dare you stick your neck out, and join the minority?

These were the questions that Jesus asked the people who thronged round him that day as he told them about the great supper and the free invitation. You are wise to count the cost. But having done so, you are wise to close with the offer. Once you're at the great supper you won't notice the cost. You will find you have lost nothing but your chains. Why not put your trust in him now, if you have never done so before? Ask him to take you and set you free, and make you an agent of his liberation to others. Perhaps a prayer like the one below might help you to clinch things. And then make sure that you get linked up fast with some of the other guests at the great supper. You are not intended to feast with Christ on your own.

A prayer

God, I think it very wonderful that you should invite me to the great supper when I have done nothing to deserve it. I have argued you did not exist. I have kept out of your way. I have broken your standards. I am ashamed of myself and astonished at your generosity. You have promised to set me free to be the self that, under your control, I could be. Take me just as I am, and use me just as you will.

Lord Jesus Christ, you have died for me. You are alive for me. I can trust you. And here and now I put my life into your hands. In your service may I find perfect freedom, and in your strength may I help others to find it. Amen.

Postscript

JESUS CAME to 'set the captives free'.[1] What is it going to mean in practice? What difference is your response to Jesus going to make to the way in which you exercise responsible choices?

I can't tell you. You see, you are committed to a person, not to a set of rules. The world is full of systems which insistently call for your obedience. But for you there is one Master only, Jesus Christ. And his way was often unusual, uncomfortable, and at variance with the accepted norms of the pious. When he was confronted by a woman caught in the act of adultery, he did not say, 'The rule book says she should be stoned. Let's get on with it.' He looked at her accusers, so smug in their self-satisfaction, and said, 'Let the man who never sinned among you be the first to throw a stone.' He began with the woman, not the hard-and-fast rule. He wanted to help her, reclaim her. Notice, he wasn't being permissive about what she had done. What was the object of the old law? Why, to stop adultery. What was the object of Jesus's approach? It was identical. But he achieved it, not by slating her, but by accepting her just as she was, and then giving her a clean start, 'Neither do I condemn you' and a new direction, 'Go and sin no more.'[2] I'll bet she didn't. In so far as I follow Jesus, then, I shall not automatically be a hanger, a flogger, an anti-divorce,

[1] Luke 4 : 18.
[2] John 8 : 7, 11.

122

anti-abortion man without further reflection. No, I shall try to act with Christ's freedom in the different choices that beset me, asking him to use me as his agent in bringing sacrificial love into each situation.

Can we find any guide-lines for our use of freedom in the New Testament, even if there is a shortage of narrow rules? Yes, indeed. Here are a few questions we could usefully check ourselves by, to make sure our Christian freedom does not turn into licence.

1. On the personal level to start with, *will it make for growth?* God's plan for me is to be so freed from self-centredness that I grow up into the fullness of humanity as Christ knew it.[3] That and nothing less is the purpose of God's rescue operation. As a responsible Christian I am not going to allow my freedom to imperil my development as a friend and servant of my Lord. It will not do for those who were 'fornicators, idolaters, homosexuals, thieves, swindlers and slanderers' simply to cry, 'I am free to do anything.' That invites Paul's response, 'Yes, but not everything is for my good. No doubt I am free to do anything, but I for one will not let anything make free with me.'[4] He proceeded to apply that, by way of example, to food, drink and sex. Notice that there was no 'Index of Prohibited Things'. Just the invitation, as Christ's free man, to see where the cap fits and put it on. 'Am I not a free man?' asks Paul at the outset of one chapter. By the end of it, however, he is saying, 'I am like a boxer who does not beat the air; I bruise my own body and make it know its master.'[5]

There has been a tendency among Christians with a strong sense of the world, the flesh and the devil, to restrict 'worldliness' to a very narrow area of life – smoking, drinking, reading-matter, films and so on. Far more serious, I suggest, is the danger to our growth as persons which

[3] Ephesians 4 : 13.
[4] 1 Corinthians 6 : 12.
[5] 1 Corinthians 9 : 1, 26f.

comes from assuming it is *our right* to get married, have a car, a washing machine, good holidays, pleasant working conditions and an ever-increasing salary, without the least pang of conscience about the Third World. This sort of selfishness is more corroding than 'X' Certificate films. 'You, my friends, have been called to freedom. But do not allow your freedom to be an occasion for the self to have its way. Rather, be servants to one another in love.'[6]

2. On the social level, we might well ask, *will it show love?* There is a discussion in the Epistle to the Romans which we could easily dismiss as irrelevant. It is all about whether you should be a vegetarian or not if you are a Christian, in view of the fact that most of the meat in the ancient world had been offered to some idol or other. The note of freedom is clearly sounded by Paul. 'I am perfectly sure, on the authority of the Lord Jesus, that there is nothing really wrong with eating meat which has been offered to idols.' But at once comes the note of loving responsibility to others: 'But if your brother is bothered by what you eat, you are not acting in love if you go ahead and eat it. Don't let your eating ruin someone for whom Christ died. . . . After all, the important thing for us as Christians is not what we eat or drink, but stirring up goodness and peace and joy from the Holy Spirit. If you let Christ be Lord in these affairs, God will be glad: and so will others. In this way aim for harmony in the church and try to build each other up . . . ' He concludes the discussion thus: 'Let's please the other fellow, not ourselves, and do what is for his good and thus build him up in the Lord. *Christ did not please himself!*'[7] If we applied that attitude to our relationships with others, the church would be a lot freer, a lot less criticizing, and a great deal more effective in creating unity and harmony in society. Why not ask the Lord to show you how you can be a channel for his love

[6] Galatians 5 : 13.
[7] Romans 14 : 14 – 15 : 3.

124

and integration among the people with whom you live and work?

This love will lead you to want to share with others the good news you rejoice in. Here again, there is no compulsion about it, no set way of doing it, but, as Paul put it, 'I am a free man and own no master; but I have made myself every man's servant' in order to win them. 'To the Jews I behaved as a Jew in order to win the Jews. To those outside the law I became as one outside the law (though I was not outside the law in God's sight, being under law to Christ) in order to win those outside the law. . . . I have become all things to all men, that I might by all means save some.'[8] No doubt there were plenty of people who said 'Tut-tut' when they saw Paul behaving as a Pharisee one day in a crowd of Jews he was trying to evangelize, and associating with Gentile street people the next day as he put the good news in terms that would make sense to them. But that is how he used his Christian freedom in loving service to the community in which he worked. In all this flexibility, 'I am not seeking my own advantage, but that of many, that they may be saved. Be imitators of me, as I am of Christ.'[9]

3. On the political level, the question is, perhaps, *how can I use my freedom to promote order and justice?* And that is a question it is very hard to answer. The Bible makes it plain that in general Christians should 'obey the government, for God is the one who has put it there. There is no government anywhere that God has not placed in power. So those who refuse to obey the laws of the land are refusing to obey God.'[1] That was not written under a just democracy, but under Nero's Rome! Even a bad government is better than anarchy. God wants his creatures to live in harmony with the order (*cosmos* in Greek) which he brought into the cosmos.

[8] 1 Corinthians 9 : 19–22.
[9] 1 Corinthians 10 : 33; 11 : 1.
[1] Romans 13 : 1ff.

But God is the author of justice, as well as of order. So what should Christians do when the existing régime is utterly corrupt? Well, that situation had actually arisen in the times when the New Testament was written. The book of Revelation is addressed to just such a situation. It advocates passive resistance, not violent revolution,[2] for, as Jesus had said, 'the man who takes the sword will perish by the sword'[3] – and that leads not to greater freedom but to less! Jesus, ironically crucified as a Zealot revolutionary, disappointed many of his followers because he refused to allow the nationalist cause against Rome or the ideological cause for the kingdom of God to tempt him to take up arms. Force is not exorcized by force. Those who follow Jesus know that violence has its teeth drawn not by retaliation but by patient, innocent suffering. That is the conviction that stimulates a man like Bishop Helder Camara in Brazil. Dedicated to the cause of non-violence, he is none the less a passionate advocate of the underprivileged and poverty-stricken in Brazil, that land of shattering inequalities. But nevertheless he does say, 'I respect and shall always respect those who, after thinking about it, have chosen or will choose violence.'

That is what Camilo Torres did, the revolutionary priest in Colombia. There the conditions of the poor were so oppressive that he saw no alternative to engaging in active and violent attempts to overthrow the régime. He believed that in this way he was in fact fulfilling the Christian law of love to one's neighbour. His aim was peaceful revolution; 'Revolution *can* be peaceful if the minority does not resist it with violence.' But if armed force proves the only way to get revolution, it must, he felt, be accepted, for 'the Revolution is the way to get a government which will feed the hungry, clothe the naked, teach the ignorant, and make possible a true love for our neighbours. This is why the Revolution is not only permitted but is obligatory for all

[2] Revelation 13.
[3] Matthew 26 : 52.

126

Christians who see in it the most effective way of making possible a greater love for all men.'

Such was Camilo Torres' considered use of his Christian freedom. We may feel that he was wrong to countenance violence even as a last resort. And in his case violence showed its self-destructive nature, for he was shot in action by government forces on 15 February 1966. But at all events he represents a Christian revolutionary who certainly did not use his freedom as a cloak either for aimless anarchy or for pietistic acceptance of the *status quo*, but sought conscientiously to promote both order and justice in his country.

We too may make mistakes. There is no one blueprint for political action in a world as complex as ours. But we too are called to seek both order and justice without subordinating one to the other.

4. On the spiritual level, we shall ask ourselves, *how can I please Christ?* What would he want me to do? How would he act in such circumstances? 'Whatever you do or say, do everything as the representative of the Lord Jesus' is Paul's crowning advice to the Christians at Colossae.[4]

It is interesting to see how Paul handled the enthusiasts for freedom at Corinth. They had a wonderful vitality and joyful sense of liberation which is sadly lacking these days in many church circles. They believed they had already entered on their reign with Christ. They had already tasted the powers of the age to come. They were free men and could do what they liked. 'All things are lawful for me,' was their cry. 'All things are ours.'

'Yes, indeed,' is the substance of Paul's reply. 'All things are indeed yours. *But you are Christ's.*'[5] You are called to exercise your Christian freedom under his control. All truly Christian freedom is marked with the cross of Jesus, the one who showed himself most free as he went to the cross

[4] Colossians 3 : 17.
[5] 1 Corinthians 3 : 21–23; *cf.* 6 : 12.

for others. That is why Paul determined to know no other message among these enthusiastic Corinthians, except Christ crucified. He and he alone was the model for Christian freedom. Free as he was, Paul knew he was under the law of personal accountability to Christ. He did what every responsible Christian does when puzzling out problems of the right use of freedom. He asked, 'What would Jesus do now?' And if we do the same, we shall not go far wrong.

So, then, we should value these guide-lines which the New Testament gives us to our use of freedom. But then, for heaven's sake, let's use it. The church has been stuck and stuffy for too long. Jesus spells freedom. 'For freedom Christ has set us free. Let us therefore refuse to be tied up in the chains of slavery again.'[6]

[6] Galatians 5 : 1.